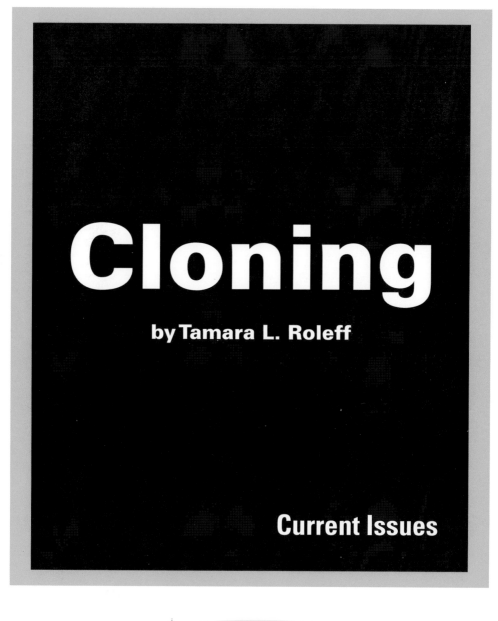

Cloning

by Tamara L. Roleff

Current Issues

ReferencePoint
Press™

San Diego, CA

© 2009 ReferencePoint Press, Inc.

For more information, contact:
ReferencePoint Press, Inc.
PO Box 27779
San Diego, CA 92198
www.ReferencePointPress.com

Picture credits: Maury Aaseng: 33–34, 36–37, 52–55, 69–72, 88–90
AP Images: 11, 16

LIBRARY OF CONGRESS CATALOGING-IN-PUBLICATION DATA

Roleff, Tamara L., 1959–
  Cloning / by Tamara L. Roleff.
     p. cm. — (Compact research series)
  Includes bibliographical references and index.
  ISBN-13: 978-1-60152-049-4 (hardcover)
  ISBN-10: 1-60152-049-2 (hardcover)
  1. Cloning—Social aspects. I. Title.
  QH442.2.R65 2008
  174'.957—dc22
                                        2008007128

Contents

Foreword

As modern civilization continues to evolve, its ability to create, store, distribute, and access information expands exponentially. The explosion of information from all media continues to increase at a phenomenal rate. By 2020 some experts predict the worldwide information base will double every 73 days. While access to diverse sources of information and perspectives is paramount to any democratic society, information alone cannot help people gain knowledge and understanding. Information must be organized and presented clearly and succinctly in order to be understood. The challenge in the digital age becomes not the creation of information, but how best to sort, organize, enhance, and present information.

ReferencePoint Press developed the *Compact Research* series with this challenge of the information age in mind. More than any other subject area today, researching current issues can yield vast, diverse, and unqualified information that can be intimidating and overwhelming for even the most advanced and motivated researcher. The *Compact Research* series offers a compact, relevant, intelligent, and conveniently organized collection of information covering a variety of current topics ranging from illegal immigration and methamphetamine to diseases such as anorexia and meningitis.

The series focuses on three types of information: objective single-author narratives, opinion-based primary source quotations, and facts and statistics. The clearly written objective narratives provide context and reliable background information. Primary source quotes are carefully selected and cited, exposing the reader to differing points of view. And facts and statistics sections aid the reader in evaluating perspectives. Presenting these key types of information creates a richer, more balanced learning experience.

For better understanding and convenience, the series enhances information by organizing it into narrower topics and adding design features that make it easy for a reader to identify desired content. For example, in *Compact Research: Illegal Immigration*, a chapter covering the economic impact of illegal immigration has an objective narrative explaining the various ways the economy is impacted, a balanced section of numerous primary source quotes on the topic, followed by facts and full-color illustrations to encourage evaluation of contrasting perspectives.

The ancient Roman philosopher Lucius Annaeus Seneca wrote, "It is quality rather than quantity that matters." More than just a collection of content, the *Compact Research* series is simply committed to creating, finding, organizing, and presenting the most relevant and appropriate amount of information on a current topic in a user-friendly style that invites, intrigues, and fosters understanding.

Cloning at a Glance

Somatic Cell Nuclear Transfer

Somatic cell nuclear transfer (SCNT) is the scientific name for cloning.

Dolly

Dolly, a Finn Dorset sheep born in 1996, was the first mammal to be cloned using an adult somatic cell.

Animal Cloning

Animal cloning has progressed from salamanders to mice to livestock to endangered animals.

Embryonic Stem Cells

Embryonic stem cells are pluripotent, meaning they can transform themselves into any type of cell in the body.

Adult Stem Cells

Adult stem cells, found in various organs and tissues in both adults and babies, rebuild or repair damaged or diseased cells in the tissues and organs where they are found. Adult stem cells are non embryonic cells.

Stem Cell Lines

Each colony of stem cells propagated from a single cell, and kept alive and cultured in an incubator under specialized conditions, is called a stem cell line.

Therapeutic Cloning

Therapeutic cloning uses the patient's own cells to create stem cells via somatic cell nuclear transfer (SCNT).

Reproductive Human Cloning

A few reproductive specialists claim that they have successfully cloned human babies, although none have been presented for verification.

Breakthroughs in Stem Cell Research

Scientists have reprogrammed skin cells to transform themselves into stem cells. Scientists have also successfully cloned human embryos using skin cells from two men.

Restrictions on Stem Cell Research

All scientists who receive U.S. federal funds for research on embryonic stem cells must use stem cell lines that were already in existence as of August 9, 2001.

Restrictions on Human Cloning

The United States has not banned human cloning, but it has placed restrictions on human cloning research. Several states have passed their own laws regulating cloning.

Worldwide Restrictions on Cloning

More than 50 countries have banned reproductive cloning.

Overview

> **❝Cloning might be the perfect sin. It just might break all Ten Commandments at once.❞**

—Terrence Jeffrey, "Does Cloning Break All Ten Commandments?"

> **❝It is not only permissible to use human blastocysts to create stem cell lines, it is morally imperative—it must be done if it can lead to saving lives or healing.❞**

—Laurie Zoloth, testimony before U.S. Senate Committee on Commerce, Science, and Transportation.

To clone something is to make an identical copy of it through asexual reproduction. Nature has been producing clones of living organisms practically since the beginning of time. Identical twins are clones of each other. A worm that is cut in half grows into two separate worms that are clones of each other. Runners sent out by strawberry and spider plants form new plants that are clones of the original.

From Plants to Animals

Beginning in the last years of the nineteenth century and early years of the twentieth century, researchers started to experiment with cloning primitive animals. Their subjects were sea urchins and amphibians, both of which have large, easy-to-manipulate eggs that develop outside the mother's body. During these early attempts at cloning, scientists split a 2-celled embryo into separate cells, each of which grew into separate individuals. German biologist Hans Driesch did it with sea urchins in 1894 to prove that each cell contains an organism's entire genetic makeup and that the genetic material is not diluted during the cell-division process. In 1902 German embryologist Hans Spemann used a human hair to lasso and separate the cells of a two-celled salamander embryo, each of which developed into a healthy adult salamander. He later removed a single cell from a 16-celled embryo; both the single cell and the 15-celled embryo grew into healthy adult salamanders. Spemann was also the first embryologist to bring up the process now known as somatic cell nuclear transfer as an "experiment which appears, at first sight, somewhat fantastical."[1] He proposed to clone an organism by transferring a cell from one organism into an enucleated (the nucleus has been removed) egg cell from another organism. Spemann's idea was indeed fantastical, as at the time no instruments could work with such microscopic cells. But by 1952 Robert Briggs and Thomas King successfully cloned a frog using Spemann's "fantastical" idea. Forty-plus years later, in 1996, Dolly, a Finn Dorset sheep, was cloned. Dolly is notable because she was the first mammal cloned from an adult somatic (body) cell.

A Primer in Genetics

A little background in genetics is necessary to understand how cloning works. Each cell has a nucleus, and inside each nucleus are pairs of chromosomes. Each species has a specific number of chromosomes. For example, dogs have 39 pairs while humans have 23 pairs. Every cell in the human body has 46 chromosomes (23 pairs), except sperm and egg cells, each of which has just one unpaired set (23) of chromosomes. When a sperm cell fuses with an egg cell to make an embryo, the 23 chromosomes from the sperm pair together with the 23 chromosomes from the egg to make 46 chromosomes.

> " Nature has been producing clones of living organisms practically since the beginning of time. "

Chromosomes are made of Deoxyribonucleic acid, or DNA. DNA contains all the genes for the organism. The latest estimate on the number of genes a human has is about 25,000, down considerably from initial estimates of 100,000 or more. Genes are responsible for passing along all heritable traits from parent to offspring, such as hair and eye color, height, and intelligence. Genes are also responsible for how the body is built and works. Genes function by producing proteins or enzymes that actually control the expression of the genes in the body. If a genetic mutation occurs, the proper protein may not be produced, which can result in disease.

Most artificially induced cloning takes place through a process known as somatic cell nuclear transfer (SCNT). In this process, the nucleus (containing all the organism's genes and DNA) from the donor cell is removed and inserted into an egg cell that has had its nucleus (and therefore its DNA) removed. Then the reconstituted cell is stimulated, either through an electrical shock or from a chemical reaction, to start cell division. The cell has now become an embryo with the complete number of chromosomes but only one parent (the donor cell). During this process, the cells and embryo are in vitro, or in a petri dish. The scientists have several options available to them at this time. They can implant the embryo into a surrogate womb where it is hoped it will develop to term, or the embryo can be allowed to develop in the petri dish for up to two weeks, at which time the stem cells are separated from the embryo to create a colony, or line, of stem cells for use in research.

Cloned Animals

When scientists learned that Dolly had been successfully cloned, they knew that the somatic cell nuclear transfer process actually worked, and they began to try to clone other animals. Scientists eventually were able to clone mice and rats, as well as cows, goats, pigs, and numerous other animals. A majority of scientists believe that cloned animals can provide many benefits for humans. For example, mice and rats are used extensively in laboratory experiments. If all the animals used in an experiment are identical due to cloning, it reduces the chance that the animals' genes will influence the result.

Organ Transplants

In addition, because of the severe shortage of human organs available for transplant, researchers are working on developing animals whose organs can be transplanted into humans. Using animal organs for transplant into humans would ease the shortage of suitable human organs. However, opponents contend that interspecies transplants (such as pig hearts into humans) could result in diseases jumping from one species to another.

These cloned cows live on Futuraland Farm in Williamsport, Maryland. Dolly the sheep, who was born in 1996, was the first mammal to be cloned using an adult somatic cell. Only a few hundred animals have been cloned since, including cows. Most cows are cloned because they produce high-quality meat or dairy products

Cloning Animals for Food

Following the 2006 announcement by the U.S. Food and Drug Administration that the meat or milk from cloned animals and their progeny "pose no increased food consumption risk(s) relative to comparable products from sexually-derived animals,"[2] many farmers will undoubtedly start cloning their prized studs and best-producing animals. For example, cattle who yield prime-grade beef or cows who produce twice as much milk as other cows are likely candidates for cloning since the clones would also be superior livestock. The cloned animals would be bred, and it is their non-cloned offspring that would become steaks and hamburgers, or produce the milk, butter, and cheese for sale in grocery stores. Since the farmer's cost to clone an animal is far more than the animal would fetch at the slaughterhouse, it is unlikely that cloned animals would end up in the food supply.

Opponents of cloning animals argue that cloning will endanger animal biodiversity and threaten the gene pool. Moreover, cloning can be dangerous to the surrogate animal because many clones develop into much-larger-than-average babies that require surgical intervention to prevent the mother or baby or both from dying during birth. Finally, cloning itself is dangerous to the clone; a majority of animal clones develop birth defects and die in utero or shortly after birth.

> **Two types of human cloning are being researched: reproductive cloning, in which the goal is to produce a child; and therapeutic cloning, which results in cloned stem cells to be used in research or to treat diseases or disabilities.**

Human Cloning

Two types of human cloning are being researched: reproductive cloning, in which the goal is to produce a child; and therapeutic cloning, which results in cloned stem cells to be used in research or to treat diseases or disabilities. While several scientists have claimed to have cloned a human child, as of April 2008 no one has proven that a human child has been cloned.

To clone a human for reproductive purposes, the embryo—formed by the fusion of a somatic cell nucleus with an enucleated egg cell—would be cultured for a few days in a petri dish, much like embryos are for in vitro fertilization. After a few days, the embryo would be implanted in a woman's uterus. If the cloning technique is successful, the woman gives birth to a cloned baby nine months later.

Should Humans Be Cloned?

Advocates for human reproductive cloning recognize that the idea of cloning a child is repugnant to many people, but they offer several reasons why parents may want a cloned child. Parents may have a child who is sick or dying, and a baby cloned from the ill child could provide stem cells that could be used to treat the child. Or the clone could replace the dying child. Alternatively, parents—whether straight or gay, single or a couple—may want a child but may not be able to produce one sexually; cloning gives them the ability to produce a child that shares a parent's genes. Or perhaps they might want to clone themselves as a way to live forever. In fact, according to Brigitte Boisselier, the chief executive officer of Clonaid, a corporation formed specifically to clone human babies, "The real crime against Humanity is to deny the right to live forever."[3]

But opponents of human cloning point out that a clone is a delayed twin of the parent, not an identical copy. The clone would grow up in a different environment than the genetic parent and would therefore become a different person. Many people are concerned about the idea of intentionally cloning a human being that is a genetic identical twin to a parent or an older sibling. They fear that the expectations placed on cloned humans to be carbon copies of their donors would prevent the clones from being seen as individuals who are completely separate and different people. Bill McKibben, author of *Enough: Staying Human in an Engineered Age*, writes that human clones would not be able to determine their own future "because in some sense their life has already been lived. . . . They would never have the sense of being their own person."[4] Those

> " Opponents of human cloning point out that a clone is a delayed twin of the parent, not an identical copy. "

who support the use of cloning technology assert that these fears are baseless. Arlene Judith Klotzko, author of *A Clone of Your Own?* writes: "Would being a clone give us someone else's story to tell or retell? . . . No. . . . We are, to use another cliché, far more than the sum of our genes."[5] Klotzko and others contend that the environment plays just as important a role in determining personality as genes.

The Ethics of Human Cloning

Scientists and researchers almost universally agree that human reproductive cloning is too dangerous to attempt. Cloning animals results in a high percentage of birth defects, abnormally large birth weights, and premature deaths. In addition, for every successfully cloned animal embryo, there are dozens, if not hundreds, of cloned embryos that do not survive until birth or die very shortly thereafter. Therefore, the likelihood of successfully cloning a human is very remote. With results like these, most researchers, scientists, and doctors believe it would be immoral and unethical to attempt to clone humans. Even in vitro fertilization, with its low success rate of just 20 percent, presents a much better success rate than cloning.

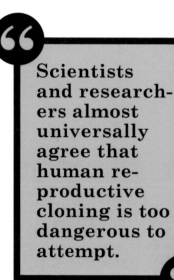

Scientists and researchers almost universally agree that human reproductive cloning is too dangerous to attempt.

Furthermore, cloning is still extremely expensive; prospective parents have other options that present better and less expensive opportunities for producing children. Some ethicists fear that cloning will lead to a society of genetic haves and have-nots; the rich who have lots of money will clone themselves while the have-nots will be left behind, becoming a genetic underclass. On the other hand, some ethicists fear that because of their commodification and their status as "manufactured" people, clones would become an underclass and not fully valued as human beings. These ethicists feel clones would be especially undervalued as genetic donors for those who want a clone for "spare parts" in case they need an organ transplant in the future, or for those parents whose first child needs an identical donor. In its report *Human Cloning and Human Dignity*, the President's Council on Bioethics explains that cloning transforms "human procreation into human manufacture, of begetting into making." Cloned children, the council argues, would be "'made to order' by their producers or progenitors,"[6] and as such would not be valued as much as children who are naturally conceived. Other ethicists counter that the same arguments against cloning were used against in vitro fertilization, which is now universally recognized as a wonderful tool to help infertile couples have children.

A Slippery Slope

Other opponents of cloning argue that cloning technology could be the precursor to the genetic engineering of "designer babies" in which parents specifically pick and choose their babies' genes. The President's Council on Bioethics contends in its cloning report, "Cloned children would . . . be the first human beings whose entire genetic makeup is selected in advance."[7] This is unlikely, according to Robert Wachbroit, senior research fellow at the Kennedy Institute of Ethics at Georgetown University, who argues that clones do not improve the human genome but merely replicate it. Cloning, he asserts, "wouldn't enable certain groups of people to keep getting better and better along some valued dimension."[8] Whatever their stance on cloning, scientists, researchers, ethicists, politicians, and commentators agree that a cloned child is a human being and entitled to all the rights and protections given to other humans.

Stem Cell Therapy

Two types of stem cells are used in therapeutic cloning research: embryonic stem cells, which are undifferentiated cells that are extracted from an embryo when it is only a few days old; and adult, or differentiated, stem cells. Adult stem cells do not necessarily come from adults; in this case, "adult" means not embryonic, or not undifferentiated. Adult stem cells can be found in umbilical cord blood, bone marrow, and blood, nasal, brain, skin, and fat cells, among others. Adult stem cells are rare and hard to find. There are very low numbers of stem cells in these tissues. Embryonic stem cells are derived from the inner cell mass of a blastocyst, an embryo that is 4 to 5 days old and contains up to 150 cells. In order to retrieve the stem cells in the blastocyst's inner cell mass, the embryo must be broken apart, which kills it.

> " In order to retrieve the stem cells in the blastocyst's inner cell mass, the embryo must be broken apart, which kills it. "

Scientists want stem cells for research and potential medical treatments because of the cells' unique ability to continually reproduce themselves. When stem cells are allowed to continue their development in the body, they are able to differentiate themselves into specific

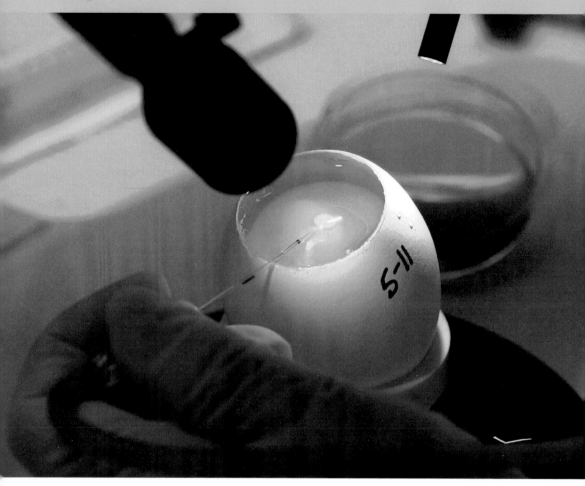

This chicken embryo (the little white circle on top of the yolk) is injected with stem cells taken from another chicken embryo. Human genes were added to the stem cells prior to implantation so antibodies would be created. This process is used to develop human antibodies for pharmaceutical use.

tissues. Embryonic stem cells are pluripotent, meaning they can develop into any of the 200 different types of cells in the body. Adult stem cells are multipotent, meaning they can develop into only several other cell types. For example, blood stem cells can develop into several different types of blood cells, but they cannot develop into brain cells.

The theory behind stem cell research is that by injecting healthy stem cells into a sick or disabled patient, the stem cells will reproduce and regenerate and create healthy cells, thereby curing the patient. Embryonic stem cells would regenerate into healthy cells of whatever area in which they were injected; adult stem cells would create healthy cells of whatever type of cell from which they were derived. And since the stem cells would be produced from the patient's own cells, there would be no fear of rejection by the body. Eventually, scientists hope to get to the point where they could use a patient's own stem cells to grow a healthy replacement organ, such as a liver. Researchers have high hopes for stem cell therapy to treat and cure diseases and disabilities such as leukemia, Parkinson's and Alzheimer's disease, and spinal cord injuries.

The Ethics of Embryonic Stem Cell Therapy

The controversy over stem cell therapy centers around the collection and creation of embryonic stem cells. The embryos that provide the embryonic stem cells are often donated by women who underwent in vitro fertilization and have excess embryos. The women are not paid for donating their leftover embryos, and oftentimes their excess embryos are discarded, since they are not needed. Many people believe that it is more ethical to use these surplus embryos for research than to throw them away. Some embryos are created by fertility clinics specifically for stem cell research. The couples who donate their eggs and sperm to produce the embryos must give informed consent, in which they are advised of the risks and benefits of donating their embryos for research. Another method of obtaining embryonic stem cells is through cloning (somatic cell nuclear transfer). Scientists take the nucleus from a somatic cell, such as a skin, nerve, heart, or other body tissue or organ cell, and insert it into an egg cell that has had its nucleus removed. The egg is stimulated by either an electrical or chemical shock, and it begins cell division.

> " **No matter how the embryo is created, some people are adamantly opposed to embryonic stem cell research.** "

But no matter how the embryo is created, some people are adamantly opposed to embryonic stem cell research. They contend that the embryo is a human life and it is unethical—and immoral—to experiment on an embryo. Since the embryo must be destroyed in order to retrieve the stem cells, they say the research kills a human bei͏ religions believe that life begins at conception. David Oderberg, sor of philosophy at the University of Reading in England, asse embryo is a human being and may not be destroyed for any purpose, any more than a baby or an adult can be. Every innocent human being, no matter how big, small, healthy, or sick they are, has an inalienable right to life."[9] It is never permissible, opponents argue, to kill a person, even an embryo, even if it is for the greater good.

Most scientists disagree with this position, maintaining that if the embryos are destined to be discarded, it is acceptable, even preferable, to use them for medical research. The Ethics Committee of the American Society for Reproductive Medicine issued a report which states, "It is ethically acceptable to derive and use [embryonic stem] cells in research to develop cell replacement therapies and to further other medical uses."[10]

What Policies Should Govern Cloning?

More than 50 countries have banned reproductive cloning; the United States, however, has no federal law that prohibits it. Congress has been unsuccessful in passing any laws banning the research since legislators cannot agree on whether therapeutic cloning should be included in the ban. Several states have passed their own laws that explicitly forbid reproductive cloning, while others permit therapeutic cloning but make no mention of reproductive cloning, and still others prohibit both or are completely silent on the issue. The United States has attempted to persuade the United Nations to ban all forms of human cloning. While outlawing human reproductive cloning has gained widespread global support, the governments of many countries feel that therapeutic cloning shows great promise and should be encouraged. The United Nations has been able to pass only a nonbonding declaration in 2005 that urges the global community to prohibit all cloning research.

> More than 50 countries have banned reproductive cloning; the United States, however, has no federal law that prohibits it.

On August 9, 2001, President George W. Bush placed a moratorium on all research using embryonic stem cell lines in the United States. Scientists who received any kind of federal funding for their work could use only stem cell lines that were developed prior to the announcement of the moratorium. In 2007 the president was encouraged in his stand against embryonic stem cell research by results from two studies that were able to derive stem cells from sources other than embryos. In June 2007 researchers reported being able to reprogram mice skin cells into embryonic stem cells. In November 2007 two different groups of scientists published papers claiming that they were able to reprogram human somatic cells to become embryonic stem cells. These announcements encouraged the president and others who believe that adult stem cells—not embryonic stem cells—should be used in therapeutic cloning research. Other scientists maintain, however, that despite advances in adult stem cell research, research into embryonic stem cells shows great promise and should not be abandoned.

The issues raised with cloning will likely become more controversial with each new development. The main issues of contention seem to be whether a particular procedure should be done just because scientists know how to do it, and which—if any—regulations should be placed on the cloning techniques.

Should Cloning Be Used in Animals?

66 It is unconscionable to use biotechnology to knowingly create animals that will suffer in order to produce milk and meat that most Americans would prefer not to consume. 99

—Allan Kornberg, "Goodbye, Dolly: Rejecting Cloned Food."

66 It's unlikely that you will eat a cloned animal anytime soon. At a cost of about $20,000 each to produce, clones are used for breeding—not for food. 99

—Linda Bren, "Cloning: Revolution or Evolution in Animal Production?"

Some types of cloning are very easy to do—with or without human help—and have been done for centuries, if not millennia. Many plants produce clones of themselves without any help from nurseries or botanists. Potato "eyes" are actually clones of the potato plant. Some plants clone themselves through self-pollination; the seeds produced are a clone of the parent plant. Scientists, farmers, and botanists have learned to clone plants by taking a cutting from the plant. Either the cutting is treated with a rooting compound that encourages the cutting to develop roots and grow into a new plant, or it is grafted onto another trunk or stem. Scientists can clone some plants by taking a scraping of plant cells and growing the cells in a special medium until they develop into a plant.

Cloning Animals

Cloning animals is a different matter. While a worm that has been cut in half will regenerate missing parts and become two identical worms—essentially clones of each other—it is much more difficult to clone other animals. Scientists have been trying to clone animals for more than a century, first by splitting frog and salamander embryos in two, and then through nuclear transfer, in which the nucleus from a donor's cell is transferred into an enucleated egg cell (a cell that has had its nucleus removed). From amphibians, researchers moved on to mice, the staple of laboratory experiments.

It took many years, however, before scientists were able to clone mice. Karl Illmensee and his research partner Peter Hoppe published an article in 1981 in *Cell*, reporting that they had successfully cloned mice. No one was able to duplicate their results for several years. In 1984 two scientists, James McGrath and Davor Solter, concluded in a paper published in the prestigious scientific journal *Science*, that their failures to replicate Illmensee and Hoppe's experiment to produce cloned mice "suggest that the cloning of mammals by simple nuclear transfer is biologically impossible."[11] Shortly afterward, McGrath and Solter were proven wrong, and scientists and researchers began to clone all types of animals, from sheep to cows to dogs and cats, and even a few endangered animals.

Advantages of Cloning

Animals are cloned for a variety of reasons: for medical research; to prevent extinction; to reproduce high-quality meat or milk products; the animals are resistant to diseases; or transgenic, they have genes from a different organism inserted into them, such as pigs or sheep that had human genes inserted into

> " Scientists have been trying to clone animals for more than a century. "

their DNA. Some researchers even cloned a pet cat and a dog. If the animals are reproduced via the usual sexual means, the desired quality might be lost, diluted, or appear in only a small percentage of the animals. When an animal is cloned, farmers and researchers are assured that only the best quality individual with the most desirable traits is reproduced. The animal is an identical copy of the original with all the same characteristics and no possibility of losing any of the desirable qualities.

Organ Transplants

Many scientists believe that cloning animals will provide many health benefits for humans. For example, cloning could alleviate the great shortage of organs available for transplant into humans. Pig organs are about the same size as human organs, and pigs are plentiful. Before such transplants could be made available, however, scientists would have to delete or "knock out" the genes in the animals that would cause a human body to reject the animal organ. Once the gene has been eliminated, scientists could clone the animal to preserve the gene's "knocked out" status. Scientists envision other uses for cloned animals. For example, scientists have learned that they can insert a gene into animals that makes them produce insulin that can be used by diabetics to treat their disease. Cloning ensures that this gene is present and available.

> " If the animals are reproduced via the usual sexual means, the desired quality might be lost, diluted, or appear in only a small percentage of the animals. "

Some concerns have been raised about using animal organs and insulin in humans. Several outbreaks of dangerous diseases, such as AIDS and Severe Acute Respiratory Syndrome (SARS), were caused when the disease jumped from monkeys (AIDS) and birds (SARS) to humans. Pigs also carry a retrovirus that can infect humans. Critics contend that the risks involved in transplanting animal organs into humans or producing proteins in animals for use in humans do not justify the use of animals in this way. In addition, animal rights activists argue that it is unethical to use animals as "spare parts" for humans.

Cloning and Drugs

Cloned mice are extremely helpful in determining the usefulness of potential drugs, among other things. Scientists have developed mice that are especially susceptible to cancer; by cloning these mice, researchers will know that all the mice share this same predilection toward cancer. When new drugs are tested on the cloned mice, scientists can be assured that the results are due to the drug's effectiveness (or lack thereof) and not due to differences in the animals' genes.

Cloning critics oppose not only cloning but also the practice of combining cloning with genetic engineering, or manipulating the animal's genes before it is cloned. Opponents also point out that cloning reduces biodiversity. If all the herds of livestock or labs full of mice share the same genes, then the entire population could be wiped out by a disease to which the animals have no immunity or resistance. Farms and researchers now realize that biodiversity helps protect animals and crops from being destroyed by disease, pests, or climate conditions.

Cloned Food

Livestock has been cloned since about 1996. A dozen years later, only about 600 animals have been cloned. One reason for the low number is that in 2001 the Food and Drug Administration's (FDA) Center for Veterinary Medicine asked farmers and researchers to voluntarily keep cloned livestock out of the food supply until it had had a chance to study the safety of consuming cloned animals and their associated food products. In January 2008 the FDA released its final report on animal cloning and food safety, and an FDA official declared, "Meat and milk from clones of cattle, swine and goats and their offspring are as safe to eat as food from conventionally bred animals."[12] (A determination had not yet been made on sheep.) Another FDA food safety expert contends, "It is beyond our imagination to even find a theory that would cause the food to be unsafe."[13]

> " Several outbreaks of dangerous diseases, such as AIDS and Severe Acute Respiratory Syndrome (SARS), were caused when the disease jumped from [animals] to humans. "

Scott Simplot, an Idaho rancher, has cloned 22 head of cattle. Some are cloned because they produce significantly more milk than the others; others are cloned because they produce prime beef, with lots of marbling and lean muscle. Simplot says, "There is nothing like a great, memorable steak and we decided that we have to figure out a way to re-create that."[14]

He believes it is a travesty not to use technology to bring better food to the dinner table.

The final report's findings were based on hundreds of studies from around the world that compared meat and milk from conventionally bred animals to cloned animals. According to the report, its researchers could find no differences between cloned animals and those conventionally bred, even when their cells and blood were compared: "Healthy adult clones are virtually indistinguishable from their comparators even at the level of clinical chemistry and hematology."[15] With this pronouncement, these food products are now cleared to be sold to consumers without labeling to indicate that the milk and meat are the products of cloned animals.

Cloned Food Is Unlikely to Enter the Food Supply

It is unlikely, however, that the cloned animals themselves will enter the food supply. Due to the cost of cloning—up to $15,000 per animal—farmers are more likely to clone livestock for breeding purposes only. Farmers are especially interested in cloning their prized animals, such as cows that develop extra lean and tasty meat or who are exceptional milk producers. It is their progeny whose meat and milk products will be sold to consumers.

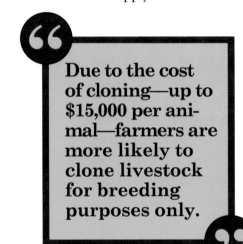

Due to the cost of cloning—up to $15,000 per animal—farmers are more likely to clone livestock for breeding purposes only.

Opponents of cloning animals for food object not only to eating cloned animals but their offspring as well. According to the Center for Food Safety, "Animal cloning is a new technology with potentially severe risks for food safety." The organization points out that animal cloning has a high rate of genetic abnormalities and warns that even healthy-looking clones could have hidden genetic imbalances that could threaten the safety of their meat or milk. Furthermore, it asserts that animal cloning is cruel because cloned animals "have more health problems and higher mortality rates than sexually reproduced animals."[16] Finally, opponents argue that cloned food should not be in the food supply because a majority of Americans oppose buying and eating cloned food. According to a September 2007 food industry poll, 50 percent of those polled did not have a favorable impression of animal cloning; 53 percent were unlikely to buy meat, milk, and eggs from cloned animals; and 51 percent were unlikely to buy these same food products from the offspring of cloned animals.

A Controversial Issue

The issues raised by animal cloning are destined to become more controversial as knowledge of biotechnology continues to expand. The fundamental issue is whether cloning imperceptibly alters an organism so that it becomes unsafe to eat. Although cloning is still experimental and has not yet become widespread, researchers, doctors, ethicists, and the general population should be prepared for the day when "someday" becomes "today."

Primary Source Quotes*

Should Cloning Be Used in Animals?

66 Asking whether cloned meat and milk are safe is not even the right question. The right question is, why clone at all? 99

—*New York Times,* "Safe as Milk?" January 6, 2007, p. A14(L).

The *New York Times* is a daily newspaper in New York City.

66 There are no biological reasons . . . to indicate that consumption of edible products from cattle, pigs, or goat clones poses a greater risk than consumption of those products from their non-clone counterparts. 99

—Food and Drug Administration, Center for Veterinary Medicine, *Animal Cloning: A Risk Assessment.* Rockville, MD: U.S. Department of Health and Human Services, January 8, 2008, p. 320.

The FDA is responsible for protecting the public health by ensuring the safety of human drugs, biological products, and the nation's food supply.

Bracketed quotes indicate conflicting positions.

* Editor's Note: While the definition of a primary source can be narrowly or broadly defined, for the purposes of Compact Research, a primary source consists of: 1) results of original research presented by an organization or researcher; 2) eyewitness accounts of events, personal experience, or work experience; 3) first-person editorials offering pundits' opinions; 4) government officials presenting political plans and/or policies; 5) representatives of organizations presenting testimony or policy.

❝It stretches credulity to claim . . . that cloning animals for food . . . will inexorably push society down a slippery slope to cloning humans. Drinking a glass of milk from the offspring of a cloned cow is unlikely to inspire you to clone your children.❞

—*Economist*, "Son of Frankenfood?" January 18, 2008, p. 67.

The *Economist* is a conservative British news journal.

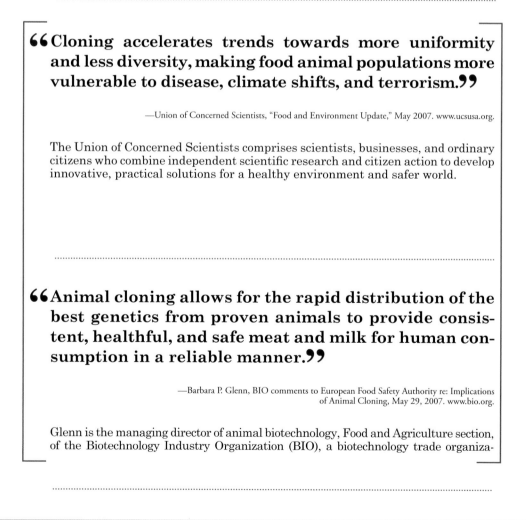

❝Cloning accelerates trends towards more uniformity and less diversity, making food animal populations more vulnerable to disease, climate shifts, and terrorism.❞

—Union of Concerned Scientists, "Food and Environment Update," May 2007. www.ucsusa.org.

The Union of Concerned Scientists comprises scientists, businesses, and ordinary citizens who combine independent scientific research and citizen action to develop innovative, practical solutions for a healthy environment and safer world.

❝Animal cloning allows for the rapid distribution of the best genetics from proven animals to provide consistent, healthful, and safe meat and milk for human consumption in a reliable manner.❞

—Barbara P. Glenn, BIO comments to European Food Safety Authority re: Implications of Animal Cloning, May 29, 2007. www.bio.org.

Glenn is the managing director of animal biotechnology, Food and Agriculture section, of the Biotechnology Industry Organization (BIO), a biotechnology trade organiza-

66 **Animal eggs could provide an essentially unlimited supply of oocytes with which to hone the techniques and skills of SCNT [somatic cell nuclear transfer], allowing more rapid progress and sparing the use of valuable human eggs.** 99

—Academy of Medical Sciences, *Inter-Species Embryos, a Report by the Academy of Medical Sciences,* June 2007. www.acmedsci.ac.uk.

The fellows of the Academy of Medical Sciences are leading medical scientists from hospitals, private practice, academia, industry, and public service in the United Kingdom. The AMS promotes advances in medical science and campaigns to ensure these are converted into health-care benefits for society.

66 **There is no guarantee that cloned animals will be 'carbon copies' of original animals in either appearance or personality.** 99

—Theodora Capaldo, letter to assembly member Lloyd Levine, April 26, 2005. www.neavs.org.

Capaldo is the president of the New England Anti-Vivisection Society, an organization that advocates for the protection of animals.

66 **Cloning means total genome control. It bypasses the uncertainties of breeding. It also improves breeding, since five clones of your best bull or cow produce five times as much sperm or eggs.** 99

—William Saletan, "Cloned Bull," *Slate,* January 6, 2007. www.slate.com.

Saletan is a national correspondent for *Slate* magazine.

"As a new assisted reproductive technology, cloning can consistently produce healthier animals and a healthier meat and milk supply."

—Jim Greenwood, "BIO Statement: FDA Announces Safety of Food Products from Cloned Animals and Their Offspring," December 28, 2006. www.bio.org.

Greenwood is the president and chief executive officer of the Biotechnology Industry Organization (BIO), a biotechnology trade association that represents more than 1,100 biotechnology companies, academic institutions, and related organizations.

....

"Pouring time and money into such [animal] clone-based research actually has profoundly negative effects on both human health and animal welfare."

—Neal Barnard, "Dog Cloning Raises Ethical Issues," *American-Statesman* (Austin, TX), August 11, 2005, p. A15.

Barnard is the president of the Physicians Committee for Responsible Medicine.

....

"Cloning [animals] will not be a mass-use technology but a way of disseminating useful traits and of creating a genetic insurance."

—James Randerson, "Descendants of Dolly," *Guardian* (Manchester), July 16, 2007. www.guardian.co.uk.

Randerson is a science correspondent for the *Guardian* newspaper in Manchester, England.

....

66 Until the technology is improved, these surviving clones carry an ethical cost in terms of justifying animal welfare concerns from the high rates of mortality throughout gestation and the post-natal period. 99

—David N. Wells, "Cloning in Livestock Agriculture," *Reproduction,* no. 61, 2003, p. 147.

Wells is a scientist with Reproductive Technologies Group at AgResearch in Ruakura, New Zealand.

66 The safety of food has nothing to do with how the animal was conceived any more than the sex of a child is determined by which page of the Kama Sutra the parents preferred. 99

—Andrew Kantor, "I'll Have a Cloneburger, Medium Rare," *USA Today,* January 5, 2007. www.usatoday.com.

Kantor is a technology writer and former magazine editor.

66 Cloning animals with superior genetics will make animal products better and less expensive. 99

—*Washington Post,* "Clone on the Range," December 27, 2006, p. A18.

The *Washington Post* is a daily newspaper in Washington, D.C.

❝As a nation we should reject any form of human-non-human hybrid formation on the same grounds for which I and millions of Americans reject human cloning: human embryos have a privileged moral status and should not be treated as raw material for medical research.❞

—Thomas Berg, "Of Cybrids, Hybrids, and Chimeras," *National Review Online*, October 23, 2007. http://article.nationalreview.com.

The Reverend Berg is executive director of the Westchester Institute for Ethics and the Human Person and member of the ethics committee of New York's Empire State Stem Cell Board.

❝The creation of chimeras [an organism that has cells or tissues from a different species] may be key to coaxing human stem cells to develop into fully functional replacement kidneys, livers and hearts.❞

—Lee Silver, "Raising Beast People," *Newsweek International*, July 31, 2006. www.leemsilver.net.

Silver is a professor of molecular biology and public policy in the Woodrow Wilson School of Public & International Affairs at Princeton University.

❝[Cloning technology] has the potential to produce products that are safer, healthier, and tastier—bacon that has heart-protective Omega 3's, say, or milk produced by cows that are stronger and thus need fewer antibiotics.❞

—James E. McWilliams, "Food Politics, Half Baked," *New York Times*, February 5, 2008. www.newyorktimes.com.

McWilliams is a history professor at Texas State University at San MArcos and author of *A Revolution in Eating: How the Quest for Food Shaped America.*

Should Cloning Be Used in Animals?

- Even after a decade of cloning research, more than **99 percent** of attempts to clone an animal still fail to result in a viable embryo. And of the very few embryos that do survive and are implanted, only **3 percent** to **5 percent** result in offspring that live to adulthood.

- It took Ian Wilmut and his colleagues at the Roslin Institute **277 attempts** to produce Dolly, the first mammal to be cloned from an adult cell.

- Of the **277 cloned sheep** embryos produced at Roslin Institute, only **29 developed** to the blastocyst stage and were transferred to surrogate ewes.

- In 2002 nearly **25 percent** of cloned calves at a research facility in New Zealand died between birth and weaning, compared to **5 percent** of noncloned calves.

- Animals created through somatic cell nuclear transfer **are not 100 percent** identical copies of the donor animals. The clone and its donor would be genetically identical only if the egg came from a female donor, since the egg provides mitochondrial DNA, which resides outside the egg's nucleus.

- A study at Tokyo's National Institute of Infectious Diseases compared cloned mice to normal mice and found that the **cloned mice died earlier than the normal mice**, and from a variety of causes including liver failure, pneumonia, and cancer.

Mice Stem Cells Created Without Embryos

Mice with a human sickle-cell anemia disease trait have been treated successfully with stem cells in a process that does not require the use of embryos. Skin cells are removed from the mice, and then genes are inserted into the skin cells using retroviruses that regulate embryonic cells. The retroviruses transform the skin cells into embryonic-like stem cells, called induced pluripotent stem (iPS) cells. Through genetic manipulation the sickle-cell gene is replaced with a healthy gene. The healthy cells are encouraged to develop into bone marrow and blood stem cells, which are injected back into the diseased mice, curing them of sickle-cell anemia.

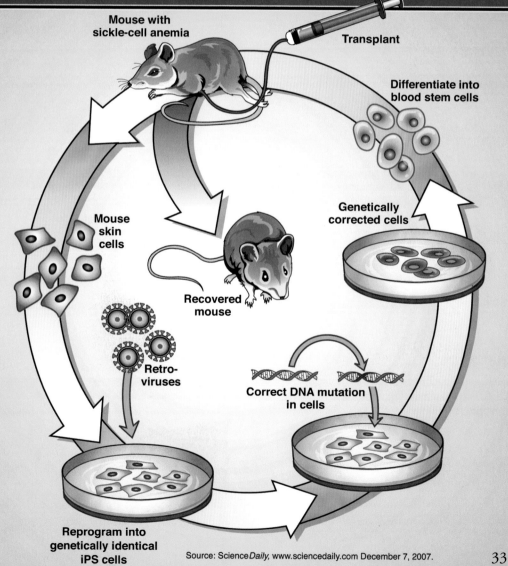

Mouse with
sickle-cell anemia

Transplant

Differentiate into
blood stem cells

Mouse
skin
cells

Genetically
corrected cells

Recovered
mouse

Retro-
viruses

Correct DNA mutation
in cells

Reprogram into
genetically identical
iPS cells

Source: Science *Daily*, www.sciencedaily.com December 7, 2007.

33

Cloned Cows Used for Breeding Only

Many people wrongly believe that supermarkets will soon be selling the meat from cloned cows. However, since it costs $15,000 to $20,000 to clone a single cow, it would be too costly for farmers to slaughter cloned cattle for the meat market. Instead, cloned cows (and pigs, sheep, and other animals) will be used in breeding programs. Clones of prized breeding animals will be used to propagate the herd using conventional breeding methods, thus raising the quality of the herd. The progeny of cloned animals—who are not clones—will be sold for consumption.

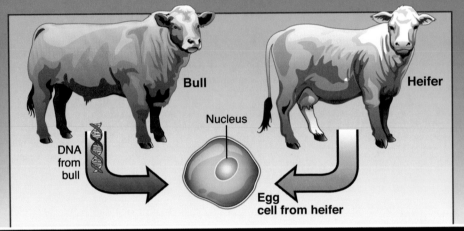

Bull

Heifer

Nucleus

DNA from bull

Egg cell from heifer

Embryos are placed into surrogate heifers

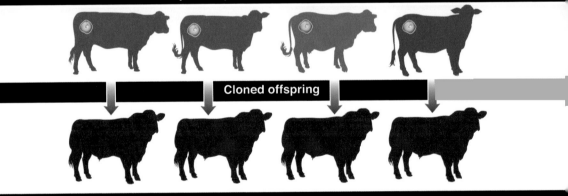

Cloned offspring

Conventional breeding methods create noncloned offspring sold for meat

Source: *Los Angeles Times*, January 16, 2008.

- Scientists can prove that an offspring is a clone through **genetic fingerprinting**, which compares DNA between the clone and the donor. Scientists concluded that Dolly's DNA matched her donor precisely. The chance that another sheep would have the same DNA as Dolly strictly by chance is 2 billion to one.

- Pig heart valves are widely used to repair damaged heart valves in humans. The valve is treated with a chemical that prevents the human body from rejecting it.

- In August 2003 researchers at the Shanghai Second Medical University in China reported that they had successfully fused human skin cells and **dead rabbit eggs** to create the first human chimeric embryos. The embryos were allowed to develop for several days in a laboratory setting, then destroyed to harvest the resulting stem cells. Scientists hope to generate a cheap and easily available line of human stem cells for research.

- The world's **first cloned cat**, a gray tiger tabby named CC (for Copy Cat), looked nothing like her genetic donor, an orange calico named Rainbow. A cat's coat color is only partially genetically determined; the random deactivation or "turning off" of genes during the fetal development also plays a role in coat color.

- In **January 2008** the Food and Drug Administration released a report in which it declared that edible products from cloned animals posed no additional risks compared to conventionally reproduced animals.

- The 2007 International Food Information Council survey found that the percentage of American consumers who are "somewhat" or "very" likely to purchase products from the offspring of cloned animals is increasing—**49 percent** in 2007, up from **41 percent** in 2006.

- The first **cattle clones** were born in 1998, followed by pigs in 2000.

- In 2008, Viagen, a gene-banking and cloning company, charged **$17,500** to clone a cow and **$4,000** to clone a pig.

- In 2008, there were fewer than **100** cloned cattle in the United States. Industry experts estimate that the number of livestock clones born by 2013 will range between a few hundred to no more than **1,000**.

- In 2007, between the December 2006 release of the Food and Drug Administration's preliminary report on the safety of cloned food and its final report released in January 2008, nearly **150,000** Americans wrote the FDA to oppose the introduction of cloned products in the food supply. **Nearly 250 scientists** wrote endorsing the FDA's conclusion that cloned food is safe.

Majority of Americans Not Likely to Consume Food from the Offspring of Cloned Animals

A September 2007 poll by the International Food Information Council found that 51 percent of Americans say they are not likely to buy meat, milk, or eggs from the offspring of cloned animals.

If the U.S. Food and Drug Administration determined that meat, milk, and eggs from the offspring of cloned animals were safe, how likely would you be to buy them?

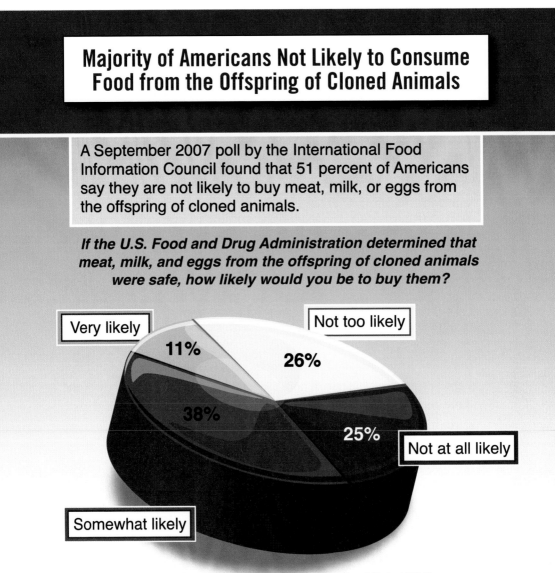

Very likely — 11%

Not too likely — 26%

38%

25% — Not at all likely

Somewhat likely

Source: International Food Information Council, *Food Biotechnology: A Study of U.S. Consumer Attitudinal Trends, 2007 Report*, September 2007. www.ific.org.

How Americans Feel About Animal Versus Human Cloning

While the majority of Americans are morally against cloning, more people approve of the cloning of animals than humans. Since 2001, those who feel it is morally acceptable to clone animals have risen from 31 percent to 35 percent, indicating a trend in public acceptance of cloning.

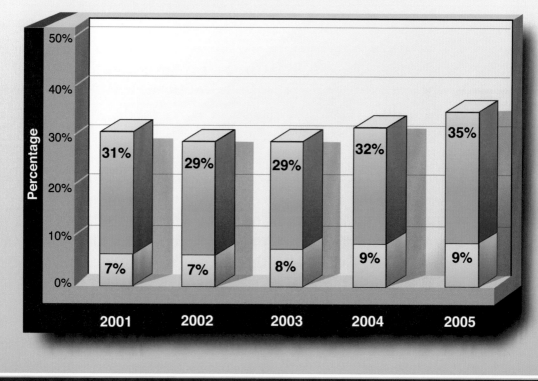

Morally acceptable to clone animals

Morally acceptable to clone humans

Source: The Gallup Organization, 2005.

Is Human Cloning Ethical?

> 66 Living in my shadow would be intolerable. Even though the reality is that a clone would be an individual living his own life, he would have to deal with the expectations of parents, family, friends, teachers, and, of course, the media. That would be a heavy burden. 99

—Ian Wilmut and Roger Highfield, *After Dolly: The Uses and Misuses of Human Cloning.*

> 66 It is likely to be a disadvantage to the [cloned] child to have the weight of the parents' memories of their previous child. But it is unlikely that this burden will be great enough to create a serious risk of life not being worth living. 99

—Jonathan Glover, *Choosing Children: Genes, Disability, and Design.*

With few exceptions, nearly all scientists, researchers, physicians, and ethicists agree that humans should not be cloned for reproductive purposes. The success rate to produce a cloned animal is very low; Ian Wilmut, who cloned Dolly the sheep, the first mammal cloned from an adult somatic cell, failed 276 times before he was successful. Since humans are much more complex beings than other animals, scientists believe that cloning a human would be much more difficult to achieve. However, a few scientists and doctors believe human reproductive cloning is a desirable and ethical way to produce children.

Human Reproductive Cloning

In order to clone a human, a human egg must first be enucleated (its nucleus removed). Then a cell is taken from the donor who wishes to be cloned. The science of cloning has progressed to the point that a cell can be taken from any part of the body—although skin cells are commonly used—and used for cloning. The nucleus from the donor cell is removed and inserted into the enucleated egg cell. The egg cell with the donor nucleus is then stimulated, either with an electric shock or a chemical solution, which starts the process of cell division. The single egg cell is now an embryo. Regular embryos produced via in vitro fertilization (IVF) usually develop for a few days in a petri dish before one (sometimes more) is implanted into a woman's womb where it continues its development; the same process would be used if a cloned embryo was implanted. The success rate for IVF is about 20 percent (20 percent of the fertilized egg cells are successfully implanted in the woman's womb and develop to term). The success rate for cloning animals such as mice, cows, and sheep is less than 1 percent, and until January 2008, no scientist had proved to be successful in cloning primates, which include monkeys, apes, and humans—despite claims to the contrary.

Difficulties of Cloning

In addition to the low success rates involved with cloning animals, critics fear that human clones would encounter problems similar to those experienced by cloned animals and their surrogate mothers. For example, the surrogate mothers of clones suffer a higher rate of serious complications or death due to an unusually high percentage of late-term miscarriages and high birth weights of their cloned young. Cloned animals are also documented to have more birth defects. What is more, many cloned animals die prematurely, so it is feared that cloned humans would not live a normal life span. Moreover, cloning a human would be extremely expensive, thus presenting the possibility

> " Since humans are much more complex beings than other animals, scientists believe that cloning a human would be much more difficult to achieve. "

that only the very rich would be able to clone themselves, thereby creating a society of "haves" and "have-nots." Finally, the President's Council on Bioethics concluded in its 2002 report *Human Cloning and Human Dignity* that it would be difficult to make human cloning safe for use in the future: "Conducting experiments in an effort to make cloning-to-produce-children less dangerous would itself be an unacceptable violation of the norms of research ethics. There seems to be no ethical way to try to discover whether cloning to produce children can become safe, now or in the future."[17] Ethicists take the dangers and risks associated with animal cloning, extrapolate them to human cloning, and reason that since cloning is an experimental procedure fraught with risks, it is inherently unethical to experiment on human embryos who cannot give informed consent.

> If cloning technology ever improves to the point where cloning becomes as safe as IVF, . . . the debate will change from whether humans should be cloned to whether it is ethical to clone humans.

If cloning technology ever improves to the point where cloning becomes as safe as IVF and is no longer considered experimental, the debate will change from whether humans should be cloned to whether it is ethical to clone humans. With the change in focus, consensus lessens. Some objections to reproductive cloning concern the individuality of the clone, how the addition of a clone will affect family dynamics and structure, the commodification of cloned humans, the possibility that cloning will lead to eugenics, and the role of God in creating people.

Infertility

Despite the risks, some are willing to consider human cloning for certain situations. Some researchers believe that cloning is an option for couples who are infertile or gay, or for single parents who wish to have a child who is genetically related to them. Those who support cloning as a way for infertile couples to have genetically related children point out that the arguments against new reproductive technologies have not changed. The same arguments that were once used against other reproductive technologies such as IVF, artificial insemination, and surrogate motherhood during their early days are now being used against cloning. These methods were once called unnatural, immoral, and against the laws of nature. Today, they are accepted as technologies that allow a man and a woman to have a baby and become a family. Someday, cloning supporters assert, cloning will be viewed in the same way and will be as safe as IVF and other reproductive methods.

A "Mini-Me"

Psychiatrists and others suggest that people who are clones would suffer from a lack of a clear genetic identity. Because clones are a genetic "Mini-Me," a younger version of the donor, critics fear that clones would be constantly compared to their genetic donors and be faced with the expectation of being a copy of the donor. According to psychiatrist Stephen Levick, the child is at risk of losing his own autonomy, of being her own person. The child will be expected to follow in the parent's footsteps. Levick suggests: "If the child is different [from the parent] then the child is a disappointment. Even if the child is different in a good way it's a disappointment. 'Gee, I thought you would be interested in music but you're interested in this other thing instead.'"[18] Levick and others contend that clones may feel, because of the expectations placed on them, as if their own lives have already been lived.

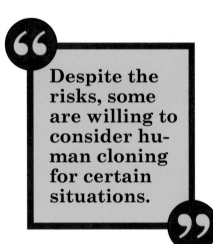

Despite the risks, some are willing to consider human cloning for certain situations.

Supporters of reproductive cloning contend that the arguments against it are irrational and unfair. Julian Savulescu, Uehiro Professor of Practical Ethics at the University of Oxford, argues that while clones have the same genes as their donors, to "copy your complete DNA is not copying yourself."[19] Environmental factors and experiences have a significant impact on a person's development. Arlene Judith Klotzko, author of *A Clone of Your Own?* makes this point with the following scenario:

> Imagine for a moment that the most crucial, transforming experience in your life had not happened. You did not lose a parent when you were a child. You did not go

through a painful divorce. You did not meet a person on a train or aeroplane who somehow gave you a vision of a different path in life—to go to law school or medical school, to become a missionary or aid worker. You never heard that political speech that thrilled you and sent you straight off to campaign for a candidate. Imagine that whatever it was did not happen. Is there any doubt that you would have had a very, very different life?[20]

Genes may predispose people to certain things, she argues, but they are not predestination.

Eugenics

Others fear that cloning would lead to the reemergence of eugenics, the selective breeding of "superior" specimens and the culling of "inferior" humans. Nobel laureate Joshua Lederberg, in a controversial 1966 article, explains how cloning might be used to improve the human race: "If a superior individual (and presumably then genotype) is identified, why not copy it directly, rather than suffer all the risks of recombinational disruption, including those of sex."[21] Cloning, he maintains, could help humans avoid genetic diseases by allowing genetic carriers to clone themselves and avoid the possibility of mating with another carrier and producing a child with the genetic disease.

> "The arguments against new reproductive technologies have not changed."

Genetic Diseases and "Spare Parts"

If both parents are carriers of a genetic disease, they may wish to clone a child to ensure that the child does not exhibit the disease. Carriers have a recessive gene for the disease; the disease is not expressed in carriers because the recessive gene is overridden by the dominant, healthy gene. If both parents have a recessive gene for a genetic disease, then there is a 25 percent chance that their naturally conceived children will have the disease. If one of the parents clones him- or herself, then the cloned child will not have the disease since the parent's dominant gene will override the disease's recessive gene.

Replacement of a Family Member

Another reason for wanting to clone a child is to create a replacement for a dying child or a tissue donor for an ill child. By cloning a dying child, the parents could ease some of their grief over the death of their child. If the child was suffering from a genetic or fatal disease and needed a transplant—for example, of bone marrow or a liver—a cloned child would be able to provide a perfect tissue match for the ill child. The parents could also save the cloned child's umbilical cord blood with its perfectly matched stem cells for use at a later time.

> " Since a clone is in truth a delayed twin, some believe family problems could arise when the parent raising a child is also the clone's genetic sibling. "

Because some parents would clone a child in order to have "spare parts" for another family member, some critics fear that clones would become second-class citizens and not valued for being their own person. Others point out that no child can ever replace another person; the clone and donor may share the same genes, but the clone is not and will not be a carbon copy of the donor.

Family Dynamics

Since a clone is in truth a delayed twin, some believe family problems could arise when the parent raising a child is also the clone's genetic sibling. In the case of a father who clones himself, the cloned child's father is also his brother. The father's parents—although technically the child's grandparents—are in actuality the child's genetic parents. Some observers theorize that such convoluted family dynamics may affect the family's stability.

Reproduction as a God-Given Right

Critics also contend that cloning would turn reproduction into the commodification of humans, the transformation of humans into products for sale. According to Sophia M. Kolehmainen, director of programs for the Council for Responsible Genetics, "Cloning would turn procreation into a manufacturing process, where human characteristics become added options and children, objects of deliberate design."[22] Cloned children would be objectified, she maintains. Instead of being accepted as a gift from God, critics assert that parents would come to believe that they could pick and choose which traits they want in their child.

> People have differing views about God and, therefore, about how God views cloning.

However, people have differing views about God and, therefore, about how God views cloning. Many Asian religions do not consider cloning an affront to God. In fact, when Korean scientist Woo-Suk Hwang reported that he had cloned human embryos (a claim later revealed to be fraudulent), he did not apologize for offending Western sensibilities about cloning. Instead, he said his cloning research followed Buddhist teachings about recycling life through reincarnation. According to Cynthia Fox, author of *Cell of Cells*, "Asian religions worry less than Western religions that biotechnology is about 'playing God,'"[23] Finally, some people believe that the right to reproduce is an inalienable right and no government can tell them how they can—or cannot—have a child.

Claims of Cloned Children

Despite the difficulties most scientists experience in cloning animals, some claim that they have—against the odds—successfully cloned a human child. In 1998 the Italian fertility doctor Severino Antinori announced that he would open a laboratory and start cloning humans. Also in that same year, Richard Seed, a physicist, said he would establish a clinic to begin cloning humans. (Seed never raised enough money to begin his project.) In 2002 Antinori claimed that he had implanted a clone into a woman and that the baby would be born in 2003, but an announcement was never made about the birth of the clone.

Clonaid is a project begun in 1997 by some members of the Raëlian cult to clone humans. The Raëlians believe that the human race was cloned by extraterrestrials. Brigitte Boisselier, a Raëlian bishop and CEO of the Clonaid project, explains why cloning is so important to Raëlian beliefs:

Reproductive cloning will enable all of us to live eternally. . . . By declaring human cloning a crime against humanity, you will just slow down an unescapable process as sooner or later, not only will we beat most of the diseases thanks to stem cells but we will also beat death thanks to cloning. . . . The real crime against Humanity is to deny the right to live forever.[24]

In 2002 Clonaid announced it had cloned a baby girl named Eve. Two years later Boisselier claimed that Clonaid had created a total of 13 cloned babies. However, no babies and their genetic donors have ever been presented for testing to verify the claims.

Worry over Benefits and Risks

Reproductive cloning presents issues that are frightening to many people. Just as the appearance of test-tube babies in the 1970s concerned many people who worried about the ethical implications of being able to conceive a child outside of the womb, so too does the development of cloning trouble those who worry whether the benefits outweigh the risks and harms.

Is Human Cloning Ethical?

> **It has been said that it is a crime to destroy embryonic life and use its stem cells to cure diseases. The real crime is to withhold stem-cell therapy from those who are dying right now or who are suffering from incurable diseases and disabilities.**

—Brigitte Boisselier, "Clonaid Team Celebrates UN Delay on Human Cloning Ban," November 7, 2003. www.clonaid.com.

Boisselier is the chief executive officer of Clonaid, a company founded in 1997 by the International Raëlian Movement with the goal of cloning a human being.

> **Cloning for research presents a new evil not found even in the practice of abortion: creating new human lives solely in order to destroy them.**

—Richard M. Doerflinger, "Human Cloning vs. Human Dignity." www.usccb.org.

Doerflinger is deputy director of the U.S. Conference of Catholic Bishops Secretariat for Pro-Life Activities.

Bracketed quotes indicate conflicting positions.

* Editor's Note: While the definition of a primary source can be narrowly or broadly defined, for the purposes of Compact Research, a primary source consists of: 1) results of original research presented by an organization or researcher; 2) eyewitness accounts of events, personal experience, or work experience; 3) first-person editorials offering pundits' opinions; 4) government officials presenting political plans and/or policies; 5) representatives of organizations presenting testimony or policy.

❝It's not the cloned child that strikes fear into our hearts. Rather it's the idea that human beings could be designed to serve another's ends, to do another's bidding, to be controlled like a puppet on a string.❞

—Arlene Judith Klotzko, *A Clone of Your Own? The Science and Ethics of Cloning.* New York: Cambridge University Press, 2006, p. 11.

Klotzko, a bioethicist and a lawyer, is the author of *A Clone of Your Own? The Science and Ethics of Cloning.*

....

❝If the statement 'Cloning is evil and should be forbidden' is defensible only by appealing to religious premises, then we have every right to ask why federal or state governments should enforce a general religious belief on non-religious couples or on couples whose religious beliefs (e.g., Buddhism) do not incline them to reject cloning.❞

—Gregory E. Pence, *Cloning After Dolly: Who's Still Afraid?* Lanham, MD: Rowman & Littlefield, 2004, p. 15.

Pence teaches philosophy and medical ethics at the University of Alabama at Birmingham. He is the author of *Who's Afraid of Human Cloning?, Flesh of My Flesh: The Ethics of Human Cloning,* and *Cloning After Dolly: Who's Still Afraid?*

....

❝[Human clones] are children born with an even clearer road map of their future . . . because in some sense their life has already been lived.❞

—Bill McKibben, *Enough: Staying Human in an Engineered Age.* New York: Times, 2003, p. 128.

McKibben is the author of *Enough: Staying Human in an Engineered Age.*

....

“**Cloning is by its nature eugenic, since it involves the deliberate production of someone with the 'right' genome.**”

—Pete Shanks, *Human Genetic Engineering: A Guide for Activists, Skeptics, and the Very Perplexed.* New York: Nation, 2005, p. 64.

Shanks is the author of *Human Genetic Engineering: A Guide for Activists, Skeptics, and the Very Perplexed.*

“**The DNA of Hitler, Einstein or Mozart in their clones would never produce Hitler, Einstein or Mozart. We are the product of our genes, but also our environment and most importantly, our own free choices.**”

—Julian Savulescu, "Equality, Cloning, and Clonism: Why We Must Clone." www.reproductivecloning.net.

Savulescu is Uehiro Professor of Applied Ethics at the University of Oxford, editor of the *Journal of Medical Ethics*, and the head of the Melbourne-Oxford Stem Cell Collaboration.

“**Whether one clones an embryo for birth, or clones an embryo for research, a clone is a clone is a clone.**”

—Kathleen Parker, "In Missouri, Calling a Clone a Clone," *Orlando Sentinel,* November 1, 2006, p. A13.

Parker is a syndicated columnist.

“**All the arguments in favour of a ban [against human cloning] describe risks that we accept quite easily and naturally in other areas of reproduction.**”

—Hugh McLachlan, "Let's Legalise Cloning," *New Scientist,* vol. 195, no. 2,613, July 21, 2007, p. 54.

McLachlan, a professor of bioethics at Glasgow Caledonia University in Scotland, is the coauthor of *From the Womb to the Tomb: Issues in Medical Ethics.*

> 66 Any use of human cloning poses a health risk to women. A tremendous number of eggs are required for creation of just one cloned embryo. 99

—David Prentice, "Should Congress Ban All Forms of Human Cloning? Pro," *CQ Researcher,* October 22, 2004.

Prentice is a senior fellow for Life Sciences at Family Research Council.

> 66 For now, the only destiny for cloned human cells is to help scientists understand and cure diseases. 99

—Arthur Caplan, "Cloning Ethics: Separating the Science from the Fiction," MSNBC.com, December 14, 2003.

Caplan is director of the Center for Bioethics at the University of Pennsylvania.

> 66 The only way that infertile children produced through cloning will themselves be able to have children is to clone themselves again. Hence, cloning could result in whole lines of individuals who are infertile. 99

—Benjamin Zipser, "Cloning People," *New Scientist,* vol. 195, no. 2,619, September 1, 2007, p. 25.

Zipser is a behavioral biologist in Germany.

> 66 A clone would be expected to resemble at least superficially physically the progenitor. . . . If one highly resembles one's parent physically I think that similar expectations exist for that person, that they be like the parent. 99

—Stephen E. Levick, "Growing Up a Clone: The Psychology of Reproductive Cloning," *All in the Mind: ABC (Australia) Radio National,* March 5, 2005.

Levick is a psychiatrist and the author of *Clone Being: Exploring the Psychological and Social Dimensions.*

66 One of the big dangers that cloning sort of brings up is that we will have these bigoted attitudes that somehow non-natural humans are second rate.**99**

—Julian Savulescu, "Growing Up a Clone: The Psychology of Reproductive Cloning," *All in the Mind: ABC (Australia) Radio National,* March 5, 2005.

Savulescu is Uehiro Professor of Applied Ethics at the University of Oxford, editor of the *Journal of Medical Ethics,* and the head of the Melbourne-Oxford Stem Cell Collaboration.

66 Banning all forms of cloning would slam the door on hope for up to 100 million Americans by outlawing vital research on some of the most debilitating diseases known to humankind.**99**

—Daniel Perry, "Should Congress Ban All Forms of Human Cloning? Pro" *CQ Researcher,* October 22, 2004.

Perry is the former president of the Coalition for the Advancement of Medical Research.

Facts and Illustrations

Is Human Cloning Ethical?

- A clone is simply a **delayed** twin of the parent, or donor cell.

- Identical twins are **natural clones** of each other.

- There are at least **8 million** identical twins alive around the world.

- In 1978, the first "test-tube baby," Louise Brown, was born in England. It is due to advances in *in vitro* **fertilization** that cloning and stem cell research are now possible.

- There are three types of cloning: **somatic cell cloning** (cloning an animal from an adult cell); **embryo cloning** (the splitting of a fertilized egg through both natural and artificial means); and **therapeutic cloning** (deliberately cloning an embryo in order to obtain its stem cells).

- The United States **has not banned** reproductive human cloning.

- In a May 2004 poll, **88 percent** of Americans said that cloning humans would be "morally wrong," even if it could be done safely.

- Respected science journalist David Rorvik claimed in a 1978 book, ***In His Image: The Cloning of a Man***, that an eccentric millionaire asked him to create a male heir through cloning. A source quoted in the book sued for defamation, and a judge ruled—and the publisher later conceded—that the book was a hoax. Rorvik continues to maintain that the story is true.

Most Americans Feel Human and Animal Cloning Are Morally Wrong

According to a 2008 Gallup Poll, most Americans ranked cloning humans and animals among the top 5 least morally acceptable issues. Cloning humans ranked third with 87 percent feeling it is morally wrong, and cloning animals ranked fifth with 61 percent of voters feeling it is morally unacceptable. The death penalty was ranked last, with 25 percent of people deeming it morally wrong.

Morally Questionable Issue	Morally Wrong
Married men and women having an affair	93%
Polygamy (when a husband has more than one wife at the same time)	92%
Cloning humans	87%
Suicide	82%
Cloning animals	61%
Homosexual relations	52%
Abortion	51%
Doctor-assisted suicide	46%
Having a baby outside of marriage	43%
Sex between an unmarried man and woman	39%
Medical research using stem cells obtained from human embryos	33%
Buying and wearing clothing made of animal fur	32%
Gambling	32%
Medical testing on animals	30%
Divorce	27%
The death penalty	25%

Source: Gallup Poll, "Moral Acceptability of Issues," 2008. www.gallup.com.

Sexual Reproduction and Cloning

Sexual reproduction in humans requires the union of an egg and sperm, each of which contain only one copy of the person's chromosomes. When the egg and sperm unite, they form a complete complement of chromosomes, and the fertilized egg cell divides to become an embryo, and eventually, a unique baby. Unlike sexual reproduction somatic cell nuclear transfer (SCNT), also known as cloning, bypasses the union of sperm and egg cell. The nucleus from a somatic (body) cell is removed and inserted into an egg cell whose own nucleus has been removed. The egg cell is then stimulated to begin cell division and form a clone embryo, which will become a cloned baby.

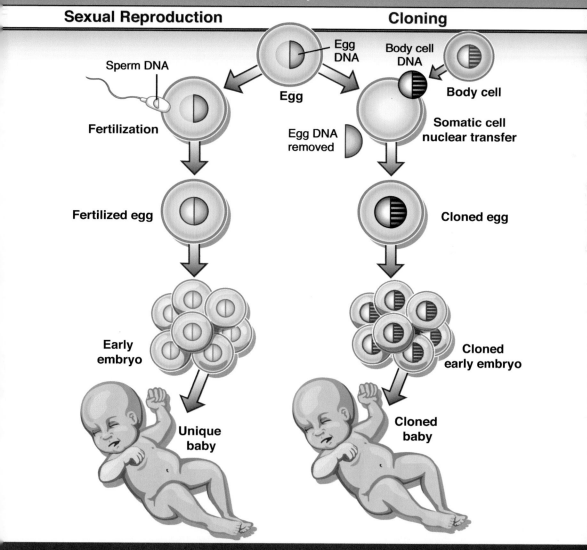

Sexual Reproduction

Cloning

Sperm DNA

Fertilization

Fertilized egg

Early embryo

Unique baby

Egg DNA

Egg

Egg DNA removed

Body cell DNA

Body cell

Somatic cell nuclear transfer

Cloned egg

Cloned early embryo

Cloned baby

Scientists' Concerns on Cloning Differ from Scientists' Perception of General Public's Concerns

A conspicuous division exists in how scientists perceive scientific concerns with reproductive cloning and what they think the public's concerns are with the issue. Scientists believe that the scientific community is most worried that such research would not be as carefully monitored and regulated as it should be. In contrast, scientists assume that the public is much more concerned with the implications of reproductive cloning as interpreted through their personal moral and ethical framework.

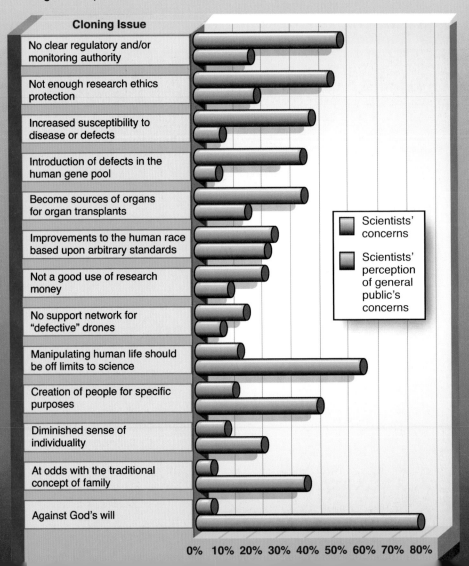

- Generating human organs from cloned cells may become reality. In 2002, scientists at Advanced Cell Technology used a cell from a cow's ear to **grow a miniature kidney**, which was then implanted back into the donor cow where it worked as a **functioning organ** without threat from the cow's immune system.

- Woo-Suk Hwang, a South Korean biomedical scientist, claimed in 2004 that he had **cloned human embryos** and derived embryonic stem cells from them. His results were later proven to be falsified.

Religion's Effect on Human Cloning

There are vast differences in opinion of human cloning when the respondent's religious affiliation is taken into consideration. In a recent study, Christians, especially Evangelical or Fundamentalists, were strongly opposed to human reproductive cloning, whereas those who were non-Christians or expressed no religious affiliation were much more supportive of human reproductive cloning.

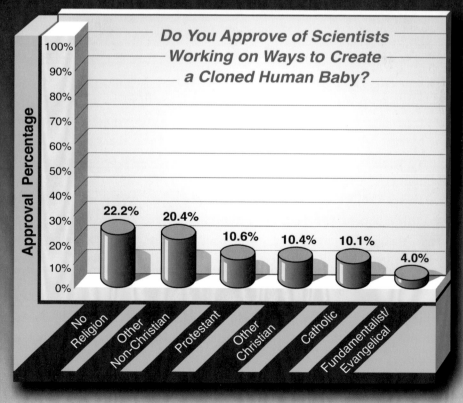

Do You Approve of Scientists Working on Ways to Create a Cloned Human Baby?

No Religion: 22.2%
Other Non-Christian: 20.4%
Protestant: 10.6%
Other Christian: 10.4%
Catholic: 10.1%
Fundamentalist/Evangelical: 4.0%

Source: Gail H. Javitt, Kristen Suthers, and Kathy Hudson, *Cloning: A Policy Analysis*, Genetics and Public Policy Center, revised June 2006. www.dnapolicy.org.

Is Embryonic Stem Cell Research Ethical?

> **Destroying human life in the hopes of saving human life is not ethical.**
>
> —George W. Bush, "President Bush Discusses Stem Cell Veto and Executive Order."

> **The potential of cloning to alleviate suffering—even end it for some diseases—is so great in the medium term that I believe it would be immoral not to clone human embryos for treatments.**
>
> —Ian Wilmut and Roger Highfield, *After Dolly: The Uses and Misuses of Human Cloning.*

Stem cells are undifferentiated cells—that is, they have the potential to develop into different and specific types of cells. There are two types of stem cells—embryonic and adult. Embryonic stem cells are pluripotent; derived from an embryo, they can transform themselves into any of the body's 200 different types of cells if allowed to continue their development. Adult stem cells do not have to come from an adult; babies have them, too. These stem cells are called "adult" because they are derived from mature (versus embryonic) cells. They are found in only a few tissues, such as bone marrow and blood, brain, skin, or fat cells. Adult stem cells are generally believed to be multipotent; they develop into the cells that make up the tissue or organ in which they are found. Stem cell research (also known as therapeutic cloning) studies whether embryonic or adult stem cells, when injected into a patient with a genetic disease or disabling injury, can regenerate the diseased or damaged tissue or repair or replace defective genes, and thus effect a cure.

Embryonic Stem Cell Research

Embryonic stem cells used in research are created by cloning, a scientific process called somatic cell nuclear transfer. In this procedure, an egg is enucleated (the nucleus—and thus the egg's DNA—is removed). The egg's nucleus is replaced with the nucleus and DNA taken from a somatic (body) cell. Each somatic cell contains all the body's chromosomes, genes, and DNA. Egg cells normally have only half of an organism's chromosomes; when the egg is fertilized by the sperm (which also has only half of the body's chromosomes), the two cells combine to create one cell with a complete complement of chromosomes and genes. Once the somatic nucleus is inserted into the enucleated egg cell, scientists stimulate it with either electricity or a chemical bath. This process fuses the 2 cells together and it is now an embryo that begins cell division. The embryo is allowed to develop in a petri dish for 5 to 12 days. At this stage of its development, the embryo is known as a blastocyst and has approximately 100 to 150 cells. Stem cells are found in the inner cell mass of the blastocyst. In order for scientists to retrieve the stem cells, the embryo must be broken apart, a process that kills the embryo.

The collected stem cells are then placed in a nutrient medium where they are encouraged to grow. While in the medium, the stem cells do not develop into specialized cells but just multiply indefinitely. This colony of stem cells is now known as a stem cell line.

Stem cells are valuable to scientists because they can be encouraged to grow into different types of body cells. Researchers hope to use stem cells to treat or cure patients with incurable and degenerative diseases such as Parkinson's, Alzheimer's, leukemia, and juvenile diabetes. Ron Reagan, the son of former president Ronald Reagan who had Alzheimer's disease, describes how therapeutic cloning could help a person with Parkinson's disease: "Imagine going to a doctor who, instead of prescribing drugs, takes a

> Stem cell research . . . studies whether embryonic or adult stem cells . . . can regenerate the diseased or damaged tissue or repair or replace defective genes, and thus effect a cure.

few skin cells from your arm." He then describes the somatic cell nuclear transfer procedure. The stem cells are grown in the appropriate culture, where they "are then driven to become the very neural cells that are defective in Parkinson's patients. And finally, those cells—with your DNA— are injected into your brain where they will replace the faulty cells whose failure to produce adequate dopamine led to the Parkinson's disease in the first place. In other words, you're cured."[25]

Curing, or at the very least alleviating, the disease is what drives therapeutic cloning research.

> **Curing, or at the very least alleviating, the disease is what drives therapeutic cloning research.**

Controversial Research

Embryonic stem cell research is controversial because removing the stem cells to use in research or treatment destroys the embryo in the process. This removal of the stem cells and killing of the embryo is what polarizes the debate. On the one side are those who support embryonic stem cell research. They maintain that a blastocyst just a few days old is not equivalent to a human being, and therefore the research does not destroy a person. Reagan goes on to say why he feels these cells are not human beings:

> These cells could theoretically have the potential, under very different circumstances, to develop into human beings—that potential is where their magic lies. But they are not, in and of themselves, human beings. They have no fingers and toes, no brain or spinal cord. They have no thoughts, no fears, they feel no pain. Surely we can distinguish between these undifferentiated cells multiplying in a tissue culture and a living, breathing person—a parent, a spouse, a child.[26]

On the other side are those who contend that embryonic stem cell research violates the sanctity of human life and is tantamount to murder. President George W. Bush, the forty-third president of the United States, is adamant about prohibiting embryonic stem cell research. He discussed his feelings and beliefs about embryonic stem cell research in a speech in June 2007: "The destruction of nascent life for research violates the principle that no life should be used as a mere means for achieving the medical benefit of another. Human embryos and fetuses, as living members of the human species, are not raw materials to be exploited or commodities to be bought and sold."[27] Because of this controversy over the status of embryos, the president banned federal funding of embryonic stem cell research on stem cell lines that were created after August 9, 2001, the date he enacted the ban.

Adult Stem Cells

Therapeutic cloning can also use adult stem cells. A few of the places where adult stem cells are found are skin, brain, bone marrow, blood, and umbilical cord blood. Adult stem cells repair and regenerate damaged tissues, and researchers hope to use that ability to treat and possibly cure diseases such as Parkinson's, sickle-cell anemia, Alzheimer's, leukemia, and diabetes, among others. Researchers also have great hope that adult stem cells could regenerate damaged cells in people who have suffered debilitating physical trauma, such as spinal cord injuries. Adult stem cells have been used, with some success, to treat some diseases and disabilities. Juvenile diabetes in mice has been completely cured using adult stem cells from a human spleen; bone marrow stem cells have helped regenerate damaged livers in mice; and paralyzed patients have regained some muscular control and mobility after being treated with nasal stem cells. However, a drawback to using adult stem cells in research is that they are rare and difficult to find; a collection of 10,000 bone marrow cells may have only 10 usable adult stem cells.

> " Embryonic stem cell research is controversial because removing the stem cells to use in research or treatment destroys the embryo in the process. "

A Stem Cell Breakthrough

In 2006 researchers in Japan released a study that had the same impact on the scientific world as the birth of Dolly, the first mammal cloned from an adult cell, had ten years earlier. The Japanese researchers discovered that they could induce adult stem cells collected from connective tissue in mice to regress to pluripotent stem cells. The next year, they took an ordinary skin cell from a mouse's tail and injected it with four viruses that turn "on" and "off" the genes that are essential for the creation of stem cells in the embryo. The activated genes reprogrammed the skin cells and transformed them into pluripotent stem cells. "It's pretty amazing," says Kathrin Plat, a researcher involved in the study. "We can take a differentiated cell and basically make it back into an embryonic stem cell."[28]

> **Adult stem cells repair and regenerate damaged tissues, and researchers hope to use that ability to treat and possibly cure diseases.**

Then in November 2007 American and Japanese scientists announced that, in separate experiments, they had reprogrammed human skin cells into pluripotent stem cells. "This is a tremendous scientific milestone, the biological equivalent to the Wright Brothers' first airplane,"[29] says Robert Lanza, chief scientific officer of Advanced Cell Technology, a company devoted to stem cell research. The implications of the research have been called "staggering,"[30] and another study released less than two weeks later shows why. Scientists announced they had taken skin cells from the tail of a mouse with sickle-cell anemia, regressed the cells back to pluripotent stem cells, then replaced the defective gene that causes sickle-cell anemia with a healthy gene. The scientists then allowed the induced pluripotent stem (iPS) cells to develop into hematopoietic stem cells (cells that form all the types of blood cells), after which they were injected back into the mice, where they began to produce healthy blood cells with no signs of sickle-cell anemia.

Adult Stem Cells Versus Embryonic Stem Cells

With studies like these showing promising results for stem cell therapy without the controversial use of embryos, some researchers, ethicists, and politicians are calling for an end to embryonic stem cell research. The new techniques of inducing pluripotent stem cells do not require human egg cells, which are difficult to obtain and raise ethical questions of their own. Since egg cells are not used in the new research, no embryos would be experimented on or destroyed, all of which are "show-stopping ethical problems,"[31] according to Laurie Zoloth, director of Northwestern University's Center for Bioethics, Science and Society. The new techniques are "a very significant breakthrough in finding morally unproblematic alternatives to cloning,"[32] adds Richard Doerflinger, deputy director of pro-life activities for the U.S. Conference of Catholic Bishops. He feels that research using embryonic stem cells should be abandoned. "It would, of course, be ethically unjustifiable to pursue the research using embryos if there were a less morally controversial way to proceed."[33]

Other scientists believe that despite the encouraging results from these experiments using adult stem cells and ordinary skin cells, it is too soon to give up research on embryonic stem cells. "I'm amazed at the ethicists' saying the problem of needing embryos has been solved," asserts Paul Berg, a Stanford University Nobel laureate who helped establish federal guidelines for human research on genetically manipulated cells. "We're not in the clear—this is a first step."[34] He and other scientists caution that many questions and potential problems still could arise with the work on induced pluripotent stem cells. The iPS cells still need to undergo extensive testing to see how they compare in the long run to embryonic stem cells in behavior and potential. Lanza is not optimistic about the comparisons. "My guess is that we'll find that there are significant differences," he asserts. "I'd be surprised if these cells can do all the same tricks as well as stem cells derived from embryos."[35] He adds, "I cannot overstate that this is early-stage research and that we should not abandon other areas of stem cell research."[36]

> " Some researchers, ethicists, and politicians are calling for an end to embryonic stem cell research. "

Additionally, the iPS cells carry a high risk of cancer, since one of the retroviruses used to activate the pluripotency genes is oncogenic—it triggers the growth of cancerous tumors in the tissue. So until scientists can determine how to get around the oncogenic properties of the virus, it is too dangerous to transplant iPS cells into humans for further research or treatment.

Still Much to Learn

Many researchers believe that scientists should continue to study embryonic stem cells, adult stem cells, and the newly discovered induced pluripotent stem cells. Learning more about how one type of cell works can be immensely beneficial in understanding the other types of cells, asserts Richard A. Murphy, the interim director of the California Institute for Regenerative Medicine. "We think there is still a lot to learn from the embryonic stem cells that will help us exploit this terrific new finding," he says. "I can assure you, there are going to be two parallel tracks of research here"[37] to study both embryonic stem cells and iPS cells. Other scientists say that embryonic stem cells are the bar to measure all other stem cells against. Robert Klein, chairman of the California Institute for Regenerative Medicine, maintains, "I think it would be insane to really desert the gold standard of naturally created human embryonic stem cells . . . when we don't know what will happen with these [iPS] cells in three or five years."[38]

Cloning a Human Embryo

Korean scientist Woo-Suk Hwang claimed to have cloned human embryonic stem cells in 2004, but his results were later proven to be fraudulent.

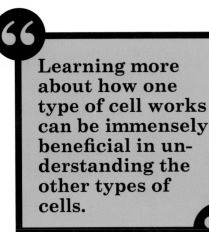

Learning more about how one type of cell works can be immensely beneficial in understanding the other types of cells.

Almost 4 years later, though, American scientists reported in the January 17, 2008, online issue of *Stem Cells* that they had successfully created a cloned human embryo. In this case, scientists in La Jolla, California, cloned 5 human embryos using skin cells from 2 men. Subsequent DNA testing proved that the embryos were clones of the 2 men. The embryos lived for only a short time before the scientists stopped the experiment. The goal of this particular experiment was to prove only that cloning via somatic cell nuclear transfer could be done. Lead scientist Andrew French says of the experiment, "No other scientific group has documented the cloning of an adult human cell, much less been able to grow it to the blastocycst stage."[39] But now that French and his colleagues have cloned a human somatic cell, the next step is to develop stem cell lines. According to Samuel H. Wood, CEO of Stemagen, the biotechnology company where French performed the experiment, "Developing patient-specific stem cell lines from the blastocysts is the holy grail." French's experiment "stops short, but it shows the entrance to the cave holding the holy grail."[40]

Contentious Debate

The debate over therapeutic cloning is even more contentious than that over reproductive cloning. Differing beliefs about what constitutes a human life and when life begins color whether embryonic stem cell research is ethical. Now that human cloning is not the only source of pluripotent stem cells, the debate is sure to become more heated.

Primary Source Quotes*

Is Embryonic Stem Cell Research Ethical?

> **Therapeutic cloning in a sense is even more gruesome [than reproductive cloning], because it creates a new human life only to destroy him or her.**

—Alfred Cioffi, "Human Cloning: Reproductive or Therapeutic?"

Cioffi, a Catholic priest, has served as associate professor of bioethics and moral theology at St. Vincent de Paul Regional Seminary, as a consultant in bioethics to the Archdiocese of Miami and the bishops of Florida, as a research associate in the biomedical labs of St. Elizabeth Medical Center in Boston, Massachusetts, and as a research ethicist for the National Catholic Bioethics Center.

....

> **Therapeutic cloning offers great promise for curing deadly and terrible diseases. Therapeutic cloning could save lives; it does not *create* people.**

—Coalition for the Advancement of Medical Research, "FAQ on SCNT (Therapeutic Cloning)." www.stemcellfunding.org.

CAMR comprises more than 100 patient organizations, universities, scientific societies, and foundations that are dedicated to the advancement of research in stem cell therapies and somatic cell nuclear transfer.

....

Bracketed quotes indicate conflicting positions.

* Editor's Note: While the definition of a primary source can be narrowly or broadly defined, for the purposes of Compact Research, a primary source consists of: 1) results of original research presented by an organization or researcher; 2) eyewitness accounts of events, personal experience, or work experience; 3) first-person editorials offering pundits' opinions; 4) government officials presenting political plans and/or policies; 5) representatives of organizations presenting testimony or policy.

66 To a public for whom stem cells equal cure, the real blow will be the realization that the simplistic picture— take a patient's genes, slip them into an egg, let the egg grow and divide into stem cells that are perfect genetic matches for the patient and transplant those cells to treat diabetes, Parkinson's, Alzheimer's—is more fiction than fact. 99

—Sharon Begley, "Reality Check on Embryonic Debate," *Newsweek,* December 3, 2007, p. 52.

Begley is a senior editor and writer for *Newsweek* magazine's science stories.

66 Pluripotent [embryonic] stem cells offer the possibility of a renewable source of replacement cells and tissues to treat a myriad of diseases, conditions, and disabilities including Parkinson's and Alzheimer's diseases, spinal cord injury, stroke, burns, heart disease, diabetes, osteoarthritis and rheumatoid arthritis. 99

—National Institutes of Health, "Stem Cells and Diseases," *Stem Cell Information.* Bethesda, MD: National Institutes of Health, U.S. Department of Health and Human Services, 2007.

The National Institutes of Health is the government's primary agency for the support of biomedical research and is responsible for developing guidelines for stem cell research.

66 Frozen embryos in infertility clinics face a fate of certain destruction anyway. The moral case against using them, or cloned embryos, which have almost zero chance of becoming people, is no less compelling because progress has been made in another area of research. 99

—Arthur L Caplan, "Does Stem Cell Advance Provide an Ethical Out?" MSNBC.com, June 6, 2007. www.msnbc.com.

Caplan is the director of the Center for Bioethics at the University of Pennsylvania School of Medicine and the chair of the Department of Medical Ethics.

66 Human embryos in dishes are not people or even potential people. They are, at best, possible potential people. 99

—Arthur Caplan, "Does Stem Cell Advance Provide an Ethical Out?" MSNBC.com, June 6, 2007. www.msnbc.com.

Caplan is director of the Center for Bioethics at the University of Pennsylvania.

66 Finding cures to diseases using methods that uphold ethical principles and sustain social consensus should be the objective of America's approach to stem-cell research. 99

—Mitt Romney, "A Stem-Cell Solution," *National Review Online*, June 15, 2007. www.nationalreview.com.

Romney is a former governor of Massachusetts.

66 Five or 10 additional years of waiting for a form of stem cell therapy that is morally acceptable to a minority of Americans on the right is too long for those who are daily suffering and dying. 99

—Nicholas Gorrell, "Breakthroughs Are Notable, but Don't End Stem Cell Debate," *USA Today*, December 3, 2007, p. 12A.

Gorrell's father died from Lou Gehrig's disease.

66 There are more than 100 million Americans . . . who might one day benefit from therapeutic cloning. . . . Each therapeutic cloning attempt would require one human egg. If it takes 100 tries per patient for a cloned embryonic stem cell line to be successfully created, therapeutic cloning will never become a widely available therapy in medicine's armamentarium because there will never be enough eggs. 99

—Wesley J. Smith, "Therapeutic Dreaming," *Weekly Standard*, vol. 9, no. 4, October 6, 2003, p. 20.

Smith is a senior fellow at the Discovery Institute, a nonpartisan, public-policy think tank that conducts research in the areas of technology, science, and culture.

66 One day we may be able to take a skin cell from a patient with leukaemia, clone it, derive embryonic stem (ES) cells, produce blood stem cells from these and transfer these back as a transplant after chemotherapy. . . . This is the holy grail of medicine. 99

—Julian Savulescu, "Cloning Research Benefits Akin to Discovery of X-Rays," *Australian*, June 4, 2005. www.theaustralian.news.com.au.

Savulescu is Uehiro Professor of Applied Ethics at the University of Oxford, editor of the *Journal of Medical Ethics,* and the head of the Melbourne-Oxford Stem Cell Collaboration.

66 Embryonic stem cells have not treated a single human patient, and only time can tell whether they ever will. 99

—Wesley J. Smith, "The Great Stem Cell Coverup," *Weekly Standard*, August 7, 2006. www.weeklystandard.com.

Smith, a syndicated columnist, is a senior fellow at the Discovery Institute and a special consultant to the Center for Bioethics and Culture.

Is Embryonic Stem Cell Research Ethical?

- A January 2007 poll by the *Washington Post* found that **61 percent** of Americans supported embryonic stem cell research.

- A **stem cell line** is a colony of stem cells that can replicate themselves in an artificial environment indefinitely.

- In **somatic cell nuclear transfer**, the nucleus of a somatic cell (a body cell that is not an egg or sperm) is inserted into an enucleated egg cell. The goal is to develop stem cells that will not be rejected by the patient's immune system.

- On **August 9, 2001**, President George W. Bush announced that researchers who received federal funding could work only with stem cell lines that were in existence at the time of his executive order.

- In August 2001 the government estimated there were **60 to 70 stem cell lines** available for research. As of early 2008, the National Institutes of Health lists approximately **20 stem cell lines available**.

- Excess frozen eggs from the country's approximately **400 fertility clinics** are a potential source of embryos for scientists to use to create embryonic stem cell lines. However, few clinics routinely ask their patients if they would like to donate their unused embryos for research.

- A 2002 Swedish study found that **92 percent** of infertile couples preferred that their **excess embryos** be used for **stem cell research** rather than be discarded.

The Amazing Ability of Stem Cells

Many scientists are enthusiastic about stem cell research because stem cells have the ability to develop into every type of cell in the body. The hope is that by injecting stem cells into diseased tissues and organs, the stem cells will create healthy cells that will treat or cure the disease.

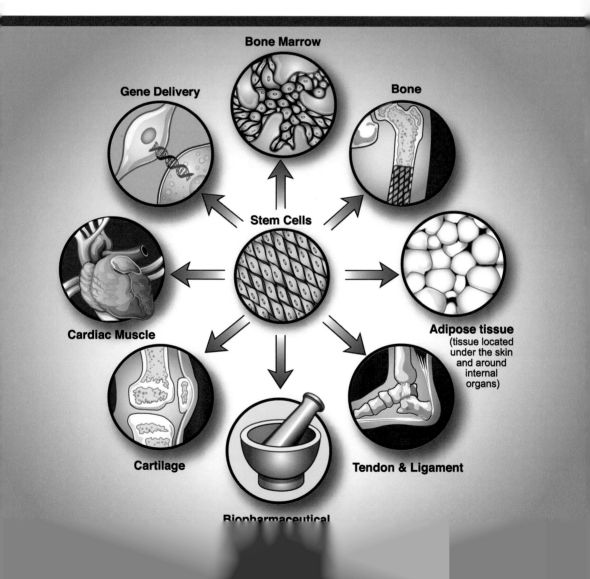

Bone Marrow

Gene Delivery

Bone

Stem Cells

Cardiac Muscle

Adipose tissue
(tissue located under the skin and around internal organs)

Cartilage

Tendon & Ligament

Biopharmaceutical

- **Stem cells** can be obtained from embryos, umbilical cord blood, bone marrow, blood, skin, liver, and nasal tissue, among others.

- Patients with over **70 types of diseases** and injuries have benefited from treatments using adult stem cells.

- Parthenotes are eggs that have not been fertilized but have still developed into embryos via a chemical or electrical trigger. Because the parthenotes **lack paternal DNA** (and therefore have only half of their chromosomes), they are unable to develop to term. Some scientists believe that parthenotes could be a valuable source of stem cells. Par-

Support for Embryonic Stem Cell Research Is Growing

From 2005 to 2007 Americans expressed growing support for embryonic stem cell research. In 2007 61 percent supported the research compared with 59 percent in 2005.

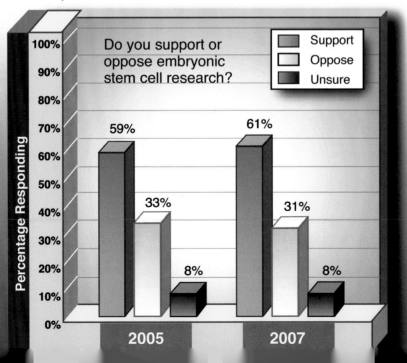

Federal and State Funding for Stem Cell Research (2003–2007)

The National Institutes of Health is the primary source for federal funds for stem cell research. In fiscal year 2008, the NIH provided $239 million for stem cell research. It designated more than 3 times as much money for adult stem cell research than for embryonic stem cell research. To make up the slack, some states have provided their own funds for stem cell research, particularly for embryonic stem cell projects that are not eligible for NIH funding.

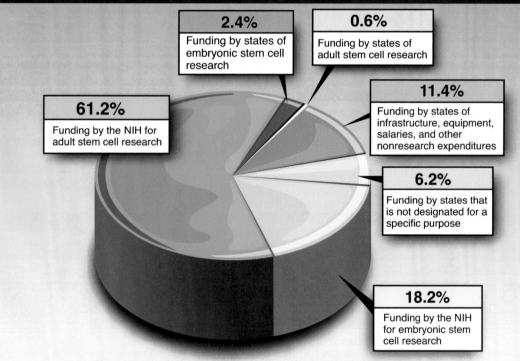

2.4%
Funding by states of embryonic stem cell research

0.6%
Funding by states of adult stem cell research

11.4%
Funding by states of infrastructure, equipment, salaries, and other nonresearch expenditures

61.2%
Funding by the NIH for adult stem cell research

6.2%
Funding by states that is not designated for a specific purpose

18.2%
Funding by the NIH for embryonic stem cell research

Source: Jonathan D. Moreno, Sam Berger, and Alix Rogers, "Divided We Fail: The Need for National Stem Cell Funding," April 2007. www.americanprogress.org.

thenote stem cells have been developed from monkey eggs, but not yet from **human eggs**.

- Two British scientists announced in October 2006 that they had grown **dime-sized human livers** using stem cells from umbilical cord blood. The livers can be used for testing new drugs, eliminating the

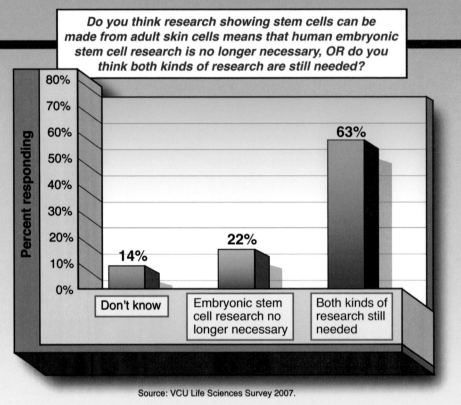

Americans Still Feel Embryonic Stem Cell Research Is Important

Although new research promises stem cell creation without using human embryos, many Americans still feel that human embryonic stem cell research should be continued.

Do you think research showing stem cells can be made from adult skin cells means that human embryonic stem cell research is no longer necessary, OR do you think both kinds of research are still needed?

Percent responding

- 14% — Don't know
- 22% — Embryonic stem cell research no longer necessary
- 63% — Both kinds of research still needed

Source: VCU Life Sciences Survey 2007.

need for animal and human research subjects. The scientists hope that the technique can be used to **grow human livers** suitable for transplantation by 2021.

- In **November 2007** researchers announced they had created stem cells similar to embryonic stem cells by inserting four genes into ordinary skin cells. The genes somehow transformed the skin cells into **embryonic-like stem cells**. The new technique does not use embryos or human egg cells at all.

What Policies Should Govern Cloning?

> 66 Our immediate emotional reactions to medical developments are an unreliable indicator of their morality. ... The 'yuck factor' needs to be treated with a great deal of skepticism. 99

—Nick Bostrom, "Human Reproductive Cloning from the Perspective of the Future."

> 66 Our feelings of repugnance at unconventional practices are warning signs. Taboos are essentially signals that a social institution is under threat. 99

—Stanley Kurtz, "Missing Link."

Just as the issue of cloning is contentious, so too is the role the government should play in regulating the technology. Cloning covers the spectrum from agriculture to health to reproduction, as does government oversight of cloning. The government must determine what effect, if any, the biotechnology will have on human health, social and economic conditions, and religious and moral values, and then it must decide what action it should take to protect those interests.

Food and Animal Cloning

The U.S. Food and Drug Administration (FDA) and the U.S. Department of Agriculture (USDA) regulate cloning in plants and animals. The USDA is responsible for regulating meat and poultry products; the FDA is responsible if hormones, proteins, or drugs are added to any food products. Farmers began cloning livestock in the mid-1990s. To reassure the public about the food safety of cloned animals, the FDA was asked to study the safety of eating food products from cloned livestock and their offspring.

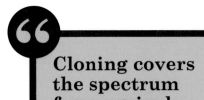

> Cloning covers the spectrum from agriculture to health to reproduction, as does government oversight of cloning.

The FDA studied animal cloning for 7 years. In January 2008 it released a 968-page, final risk assessment report on the safety of animal cloning. The FDA reviewed hundreds of scientific papers from peer-reviewed journals, assessed unpublished and raw data from various studies, and reviewed public comments generated in response to its risk assessment draft report released in 2006. In the end, the FDA concludes, "Extensive evaluation of the available data has not identified any subtle hazards that might indicate food consumption risks in healthy clones of cattle, swine, or goats."[41] Furthermore, it finds:

> There are no biologically significant differences in the composition of milk derived from clone and non-clone cattle. Additionally, data from one report show no difference in allergenic potential for meat or milk derived from clone cattle compared to meat or milk from non-clone comparators, and neither meat nor milk from clone or non-clone cattle induced mutations *in vitro.*[42]

The FDA reported that the same findings hold true for the offspring of cloned cattle, pigs, and goats (not enough data was available to evaluate the food safety of cloned sheep or their progeny.)

The "Yuck" Factor

Because it costs ranchers up to $20,000 to clone an animal—far more than ranchers could get for the animal at the slaughterhouse—consumers will have a hard time finding meat or milk from cloned livestock at their local grocery stores. Cloning advocates say the whole purpose of cloning livestock is not to eat the cloned animals, but instead the calves, piglets, and milk they produce. "Most consumers will never eat a cloned animal,"[43] asserts Gregory Jaffe, director of the Biotechnology Project at the Center for Science in the Public Interest. His statement is one to which cloning opponents heartily agree, citing the "yuck factor"—the repugnance many people feel at the thought of consuming cloned food products. "When the immediate reaction is 'yuck,' boy, you better watch out putting that in the food supply,"[44] maintains Carol Tucker Foreman, director of food policy at the Consumer Federation of America, in Washington.

The Controversy over Labeling

To keep cloned food products out of consumers' refrigerators, opponents of cloned livestock contend that all food that comes from cloned animals should be labeled as such. In support of that goal, Senator Barbara A. Mikulski from Maryland reintroduced a bill in Congress that would require all food from cloned animals to be labeled "THIS PRODUCT IS FROM A CLONED ANIMAL OR ITS PROGENY." (An earlier attempt to pass the bill failed.) Mikulski says her bill is necessary because, "The public deserves to know if their food comes from a cloned animal. . . . If cloned food is safe, let it onto the market, but give consumers the information they need to avoid these products if they choose to. We need to let Americans—many of whom find this repugnant—speak with their dollars and choose the food that they feel confident is safe."[45] Without labeling, consumers have no way to avoid cloned food products, she contends, and no way is provided to track or recall the food if a problem is discovered.

> " Cloning opponents [cite] the "yuck factor"— the repugnance many people feel at the thought of consuming cloned food products. "

Several food manufacturers, suppliers, and supermarkets, such as Ben & Jerry's Ice Cream, Dean Foods, and Whole Food Market, have said they will not carry or sell cloned products from cloned foods. Consumer advocates assert that if cloned food is not labeled, food suppliers and manufacturers will have a hard time avoiding the food and proving to questioning consumers that their foods are clone-free. Furthermore, the conservative British news journal *Economist* contends, "If the industry is so confident about the merits of its products, it should not be afraid to label them."[46]

Advocates of cloning animals counter, however, that requiring labels on food products from the progeny of cloned animals is unnecessary. The progeny themselves are not cloned; they were conceived either by artificial insemination, an acceptable and unremarkable practice in animal husbandry, or via normal sexual reproduction. The progeny of cloned animals (and cloned animals themselves) are indistinguishable from the progeny of naturally produced animals. In response to claims that cloned animals are unhealthy and die at young ages, supporters of animal cloning counter that animals who are sick, unhealthy, and who die at a young age do not become a part of the food supply, and clones who do survive into adulthood are just as healthy as other animals. Finally, animal cloning supporters assert, requiring labels on cloned animal products "would probably only cause more misapprehension about their safety."[47]

Tracking Cloned Animal Products

Other opponents suggest that all cloned products be tracked as they make their way through the food chain so that they can be pulled from the shelves if necessary. Seeing the handwriting on the wall, two of the major private cloning companies—Viagen and TransOva Genetics—have instituted a tracking system for cloned animals. An electronic identification number will be attached to each cloned animal's ear and entered into a registry. Viagen and TransOva will charge the owners of the cloned animal a deposit of about twice the animal's market value. The deposit will be returned to the owners when they show that the animal was sold to a company that accepts cloned animals. However, the progeny of cloned animals will not be tracked. According to Mark Walton, president of Viagen, his company will not track the offspring of clones because "The progeny aren't clones, so there's really nothing to track."[48]

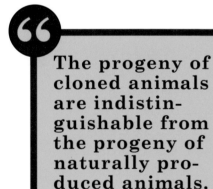

> The progeny of cloned animals are indistinguishable from the progeny of naturally produced animals.

Taking a Stand on Stem Cell Research

When Ian Wilmut and his colleagues announced in 1997 that they had cloned Dolly, a Finn Dorset sheep, using somatic cell nuclear transfer techniques, their goal was to help farmers improve their livestock. However, the world immediately focused on the possibility of using the technology to clone humans. While acknowledging that cloning holds much promise for advances in crops, livestock, and medical treatments, Bill Clinton, who was president at the time of Dolly's announcement, asserts that the new knowledge also presents a heavy responsibility for science and society:

> " Most Americans find cloning morally repugnant and support legislation that would ban it. "

> The recent breakthrough in animal cloning is one that could yield enormous benefits, enable us to reproduce the most productive strains of crop and livestock, holding out the promise of revolutionary new medical treatments and cures, helping to unlock the greatest secrets of the genetic code. But like the splitting of the atom, this is a discovery that carries burdens as well as benefits.[49]

The president then formed the National Bioethics Advisory Commission (NBAC) to study the ethical and legal issues surrounding human reproductive and therapeutic cloning. The NBAC concluded that significant risks were involved with cloning a human embryo or child and that "at this time it is morally unacceptable for anyone in the public or private sector, whether in a research or a clinical setting, to attempt to create a child using . . . cloning."[50] It recommended a moratorium on using federal funds for human cloning research and that Congress pass a law prohibiting human reproductive cloning.

A Moratorium on Research Funding

Then in the summer of 2001 came news that scientists at the Jones Institute for Reproductive Medicine in Virginia had created human embryos for research purposes. Previously, researchers had used surplus embryos from fertility clinics. No one before had deliberately created embryos on which to experiment—or at least, they had not admitted they had done so. Americans recoiled at this news, and in a televised speech on August 9, 2001, President George W. Bush announced new restrictions on research using human embryos and stem cell lines. He said that while "embryonic stem cell research offers both great promise and great peril," he was placing a moratorium on federal funds for research that involved destroying human embryos: "While we must devote enormous energy to conquering disease, it is equally important that we pay attention to the moral concerns raised by the new frontier of human embryo stem cell research. Even the most noble ends do not justify any means."[51] Under the new moratorium, Bush announced that scientists would still be able to do research on stem cell lines that had been created prior to August 9, 2001, but the federal government would no longer provide funds for any research on embryonic stem cells created after that date. The president estimated there were 60 stem cell lines available for research; however, the number has steadily declined since then. According to the National Institutes of Health (which regulates stem cell lines), about 20 stem cell lines remain in 2008.

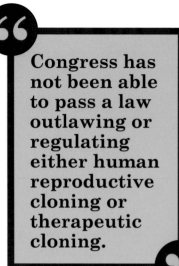

> Congress has not been able to pass a law outlawing or regulating either human reproductive cloning or therapeutic cloning.

The restriction means that while scientists can still clone human embryos and create embryonic stem cell lines, they cannot use federal money to support the research in any way. Federal funds cannot be used to pay for or maintain equipment, buildings, or employee salaries; for example, if a scientist works in a university building built partially with federal funds or grants, no research can be done on human embryonic stem cell lines created after August 9, 2001. Therefore, many scientists who want to pursue such research must set up entire new laboratories, all paid for with private, nonfederal funds.

The Debate over Cloning

Most Americans find cloning morally repugnant and support legislation that would ban it. Supporters of a ban point to the high mortality rate and high percentage of birth defects in animals and note that it would be unethical to experiment on humans with such a low rate of success. However, a few maverick scientists have announced that cloning presents hope for some couples to have their own genetically related child, and that they would attempt to clone—or had already successfully cloned—a human baby for their clients. None of these claims has ever been verified by outside sources.

Polls show, however, that a majority of Americans support embryonic stem cell research. According to many scientists, stem cell research shows great promise for treating genetic diseases; in their opinion, restricting funds for research delays the discovery of a cure. On the other hand, pro-life activists and other conservatives maintain that harvesting embryonic stem cells "involves the killing of human embryos."[52] There is no benefit that justifies their deaths, they argue.

Despite continued calls for federal legislation on human cloning, Congress has not been able to pass a law outlawing or regulating either human reproductive cloning or therapeutic cloning. In 2006 and 2007 Congress sent a bill to Bush that would have given federal funds to scientists to create new stem cell lines from surplus embryos. Both bills were vetoed by the president.

> " Both reproductive and therapeutic cloning are still legal under federal laws, with individual states making up their own—and contradictory—legislation. "

State Regulation

To fill the void left by Congress, a majority of states have passed their own laws on cloning. However, many researchers and policy makers think it is imperative that the federal government set national policy for cloning and stem cell research. To allow states to develop their own regulations will lead "to a patchwork quilt of regulations that discourages collaboration and slows research,"[53] according to a report by the Center for American Progress, a progressive think tank in Washington, D.C. Giving the responsibility to the states, the report continues, will result in conflicting regulations from state to state and differing research standards. In addition collaborative research between scientists in different states will be hampered because what is legal in one state may be illegal in the other.

The reality of state laws seems to support the Center's conclusion. More than 50 percent of the states in the union—31—regulate research on human embryos and fetal tissue. Fifteen states have banned human reproductive cloning. Some states (Arkansas, Indiana, Michigan, North Dakota, and South Dakota) have outlawed embryonic stem cell research as well as human reproductive cloning. Louisiana has banned research that uses embryos that were created in fertility clinics.

Several states have stepped up to provide funds and facilities for stem cell research. As of early 2008, seven states—California, Connecticut, Illinois, Maryland, New Jersey, New York, and Wisconsin—provide funding for stem cell research, and Massachusetts may join them in 2008 but at the time of publication had not. In 2006 Missouri voters passed a constitutional amendment ensuring that cloning and stem cell research techniques would remain legal. Missouri legislators unsuccessfully attempted to repeal the amendment in 2007, although they were able to block funding for the University of Missouri on the grounds it might be used for embryonic research.

Lack of Consensus

While politicians, ethicists, and most researchers seem content with a ban on reproductive cloning, there is no consensus on cloning for research purposes. The result is that both reproductive and therapeutic cloning are still legal under federal laws, with individual states making up their own—and contradictory—legislation.

What Policies Should Govern Cloning?

66 Consumers should have the right to know whether their food was raised in a way they deem acceptable. Only clear and complete labeling of all food products, beyond today's incomplete and sometimes misleading tags, can bring this about—and not just for cloned products. 99

—*Scientific American,* "The Beef with Cloned Meat," vol. 296, no. 3, March 2007, p. 8.

Scientific American is a monthly popular science magazine that publishes articles about new and innovative research for the amateur and lay audience.

66 One oft-cited proposal for reassuring the public—mandatory labeling of clonal products—would probably only cause more misapprehension about their safety. 99

—*Washington Post,* "What's the Beef?" February 1, 2008, p. A20.

The *Washington Post* is a daily newspaper in Washington, D.C.

Bracketed quotes indicate conflicting positions.

* Editor's Note: While the definition of a primary source can be narrowly or broadly defined, for the purposes of Compact Research, a primary source consists of: 1) results of original research presented by an organization or researcher; 2) eyewitness accounts of events, personal experience, or work experience; 3) first-person editorials offering pundits' opinions; 4) government officials presenting political plans and/or policies; 5) representatives of organizations presenting testimony or policy.

"Animals found with superior growth rates and disease resistance will see their genes spread around [via cloning] on a more consistent basis. And that could see real reduction or even eliminations in the use of growth hormones and antibiotics."

—Will Verboven, "Make That Cloned, Please," *Western Standard*, February 12, 2007, p. 34.

Verboven is a Canadian columnist who specializes in agricultural issues.

"Defects in clones are common, and cloning scientists warn that even small imbalances in clones could lead to hidden food safety problems in clones' milk or meat."

—Center for Food Safety, "Cloned Animals," January 2008. www.centerforfoodsafety.org.

The Center for Food Safety is a public interest and environmental advocacy organization whose purpose is to challenge food production technologies and promote sustainable alternatives.

"There's no doubt that cloned beef is safe to eat. . . . There's no reason to believe that meat coming from clones or their progeny is any different from traditional products."

—Irina Polejaeva, interview with Megan Miller, "Cloned Beef: It's What's for Dinner," *Popular Science*, September 2006, p. 44.

Polejaeva is the vice president of Advanced Reproductive Technologies at ViaGen, a Texas company that clones livestock. Miller is the online editor for *Popular Science* magazine.

66 Our failed stem cell policy has significantly hampered research in the U.S., and could have a detrimental effect on our efforts to find life-saving cures and remain the world leader in biomedical research. 99

—Jonathan Moreno, Sam Berger, and Alix Rogers, "Divided We Fail: The Need for National Stem Cell Funding: An Analysis of State and Federal Funding for Stem Cell Research," April 2007. www.americanprogress.org.

Moreno is a senior fellow at the Center for American Progress and director of the Progressive Bioethics Initiative. Berger is a research assistant at the Center for American Progress. Rogers was a bioethics intern at the Center for American Progress at the time this report was written.

66 The limited amount of funding from private sources will be unable to keep pace with the needs of the stem cell research community. Less restricted availability of federal funds for human embryonic stem cell research would certainly accelerate progress in this field, and improve the health of the American people in the long-term. 99

—International Society for Stem Cell Research, "FAQ: Why Is U.S. Federal Funding Important for Stem Cell Research?" February 22, 2005. www.isscr.org.

ISSCR is a nonprofit organization that promotes and fosters the exchange and dissemination of information and ideas relating to stem cells, encourages the general field of research involving stem cells, and promotes professional and public education in all areas of stem cell research and application.

66 Because of President Bush's restrictions, some of our best and brightest scientists are leaving the United States to work overseas in countries that have embraced the promise of comprehensive stem cell research. 99

—Dianne Feinstein, "Senator Feinstein Urges Passage of the Stem Cell Research Enhancement Act," July 17, 2006. http://feinstein.senate.gov.

Feinstein is a Democratic senator from California.

66 At the deepest level, cloning should be prohibited because it turns procreation into a species of manufacture.
It treats a child-to-be as an object of production.99

—John F. Kilner and Robert P. George, "Human Cloning: What's at Stake," October 8, 2004. www.cbhd.org.

Kilner is senior scholar at the Center for Bioethics & Human Dignity and Frank-
lin Forman Chair of Ethics at Trinity International University. George is Mc-
Cormick Professor of Jurisprudence and director of the James Madison Program
in American Ideals and Institutions at Princeton University and a member of the
President's Council on Bioethics.

66 Extending the moratorium [on selling cloned animals]
is unnecessary. American farmers and the food industry have proven perfectly capable of segregating foods
from various new and old production systems when-
ever a genuine consumer demand for it exists.99

—Gregory Conko, "Where's the Beef?" *American Spectator,* January 24, 2008. www.spectator.org.

Conko is a senior fellow at the Competitive Enterprise Institute and the coauthor of
The Frankenfood Myth: How Protest and Politics Threaten the Biotech Revolution.

66 Even if all embryonic-stem-cell research stopped to-
morrow, this far larger mass slaughter of embryos [by
discarding or indefinitely freezing embryos at in vitro
fertilization clinics] would continue. There is no political effort to stop it.99

—Michael Kinsley, "Why Science Can't Save the GOP," *Time,* December 10, 2007, p. 36.

Kinsley is a syndicated columnist and political commentator.

❝In the *context of biomedical research,* we now see nothing objectionable in the practice of inserting human stem cells into animals—though we admit that this is a scientifically and morally complicated matter. But in the *context of procreation . . .* we believe that the ethical concerns raised by violating that boundary are especially acute.❞

—President's Council on Bioethics, *Reproduction and Responsibility: The Regulation of New Biotechnologies,* March 2004. www.bioethics.gov.

The President's Council on Bioethics was formed by President George W. Bush in 2001 to advise him on bioethical issues that may emerge as a result in advances in biomedical science.

❝An embryo whose cells have human nuclei and rabbit mitochondria is not a monster. If its brief existence helps, directly or indirectly, to save lives, permission to create it should be given.❞

—*Economist,* "Clones to the Right of Me, Jokers to the Left: Stem Cell Research," January 13, 2007, p. 13.

The *Economist* is a conservative British news journal.

❝We cannot stop research into enhancing ourselves without also halting research focused on healing the sick and injured. If we are to ban such improvements to our quality of life, we had better have strong evidence that the research poses a greater threat to society than the medical benefits it brings.❞

—Ramez Naam, *More than Human: Embracing the Promise of Biological Enhancement.* New York: Broadway Books, 2005, p. 5.

Naam is the author of *More than Human: Embracing the Promise of Biological Enhancement* and the 2005 recipient of the HG Wells Award for Contributions to Transhumanism, awarded by the World Transhumanist Association.

66 If we are to prevent an escalating and potentially catastrophic spiral of human genetic modification, we will need global bans on both reproductive human cloning and inheritable genetic modification. The bans need to be global to prevent the establishment of eugenic tourism. **99**

—Center for Genetics and Society, "Policies: The Minimal Critical Policy Regime," July 21, 2004. www.genetics-and-society.org.

The Center for Genetics and Society supports benign and beneficent medical applications of the new human genetic and reproductive technologies and opposes those applications that objectify and commodify human life and threaten to divide human society.

66 States lack the revenue, infrastructure, and incentives to properly promote stem cell research on their own, especially with federal policies that limit collaboration, impede their funding, and fail to provide regulatory guidelines. **99**

—Sam Berger, "Keep the Focus on the Feds," April 27, 2007. www.bioethicsforum.org.

Berger is a researcher at the Center for American Progress Action Fund, a progressive think tank that believes the government should champion the common good over narrow self-interest.

What Policies Should Govern Cloning?

- In **2008 the Food and Drug Administration** released a study that found no threat to human health from food products derived from cloned animals or their offspring. In keeping with this finding, the FDA has said it will not require cloned food products to be labeled as such.

- The U.S. government limits federal funding for stem cell research to adult stem cells and a few lines of embryonic stem cells that were developed before **August 9, 2001**.

- There are **no restrictions** on embryonic stem cell research that is privately funded.

- California voters passed Proposition 71 in 2004 which provides **$3 billion over 10 years** for stem cell research. It is the largest state-supported scientific research program in the nation.

- In March 2005 the United Nations General Assembly approved a nonbinding **Declaration on Human Cloning**, in which member states were called on to adopt all measures necessary to "prohibit all forms of human cloning inasmuch as they are incompatible with human dignity and the protection of human life."

- The nonbinding U.N. Declaration on Human Cloning passed with **84 members voting in favor**, 34 against, and 37 abstentions. Australia, Germany, Mexico, the **United States**, and many Catholic and Muslim countries voted in favor of the declaration; among the countries voting against it were **Canada**, China, France, the United Kingdom, and the Republic of Korea, who argued that therapeutic cloning had the potential to help develop treatments for a variety of diseases.

- As of the end of 2007, **more than 50 countries** have banned human reproductive cloning.

- **Fifteen states** have banned all or some forms of human cloning.

- Missouri residents **passed Amendment 2 in 2006**, which prevents the state legislature from restricting treatment or research for embryonic

Americans Declare Solid Support for Stem Cell Research

A Pew Forum survey indicated a clear majority (56 percent) say it is more important to continue stem cell research that might produce new medical cures than to avoid destroying the human embryo used in the research. Nearly 32 percent say it is more important to avoid destroying the potential life of human embryos. In the past 5 years, the proportion favoring stem cell research has increased 12 percentage points, with most of those gains occurring before 2004.

Is it more important to . . .

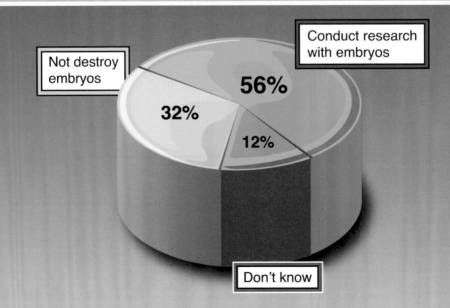

Not destroy embryos

Conduct research with embryos

56%

32%

12%

Don't know

Source: The Pew Forum on Religion and Public Life, August 3, 2006. http://pewforum.org.

Laws on Cloning Vary Worldwide

An international survey of cloning policies reveals that many countries with a strong Christian tradition ban human cloning for research, while countries with non-Christian traditions, such as Hindu or Buddhist, are more likely to support human embryo cloning for research.

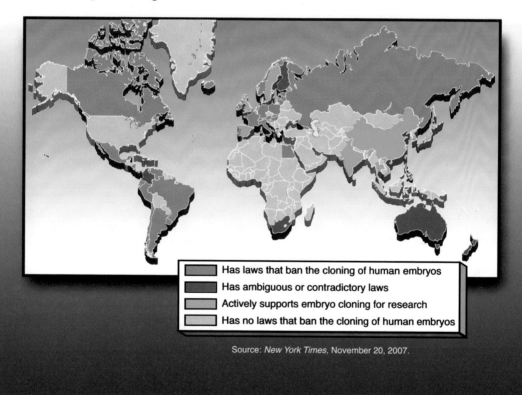

- Has laws that ban the cloning of human embryos
- Has ambiguous or contradictory laws
- Actively supports embryo cloning for research
- Has no laws that ban the cloning of human embryos

Source: *New York Times*, November 20, 2007.

stem cells that is permitted by federal law. However, the amendment prohibits human reproductive cloning.

- At least **44 bills to ban human cloning** have been introduced into the U.S. Congress since 1997, although none has passed. Congress sent a bill to President George W. Bush in 2006 and 2007 that would have funded **therapeutic cloning** research. He vetoed both bills.

Support for Unrestricted Government-Funded Stem Cell Research Is Growing

In a recent *USA Today*/Gallup Poll 1,007 adults were asked the following question:

"As you may know, the federal government currently provides very limited funding for medical research that uses stem cells obtained from human embryos. Which would you prefer the government to do: place no restrictions on government funding of stem cell research, ease the current restrictions to allow more stem cell research, keep the current restrictions in place, or should the government not fund stem cell research at all?"

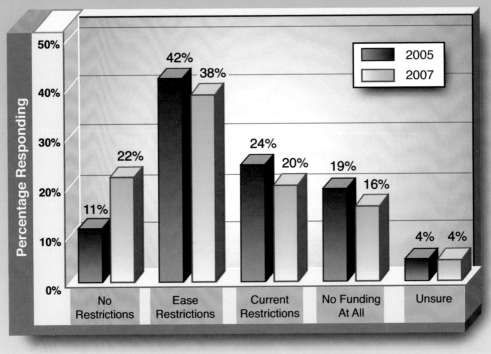

Source: *USA Today*/Gallup Poll, April 2007. www.gallup.com.

- In **September 2007** the Human Fertilization and Embryology Authority in Great Britain approved a three-year license that permits scientists to use **cow eggs**—in which **human DNA** has been inserted via somatic cell nuclear transfer—to produce human embryos for human embryonic stem cell research. The hybrid embryos would be **99.9 percent human**; the only bovine DNA would be outside the nucleus of the cell.

Key People and Advocacy Groups

Severino Antinori: Antinori is an Italian specialist in human fertility who has helped postmenopausal women give birth, including a 63-year-old woman in 1994 and a 62-year-old woman in 2006. He has also claimed to have cloned humans, but has not provided proof.

Brigitte Boisselier: A Raëlian and chief executive officer of Clonaid, Boisselier claimed in 2002 that Clonaid had cloned a human baby. No proof was ever offered to support her claim.

Louise Brown: Brown is the world's first "test-tube baby," the result of in vitro fertilization, in which the egg is fertilized with sperm outside the womb, then inserted into the uterus, where it may implant itself and result in pregnancy.

George W. Bush: Bush is the forty-third president of the United States. In 2001 he announced a moratorium on funding for embryonic stem cell research. The first veto of his presidency was in 2006 on a bill that would have provided federal funding for embryonic stem cell research. He vetoed the bill again in 2007.

Clonaid: Clonaid is a project established by Claude Vorilhon, now known as Raël, to clone human beings.

Francis Crick: Crick is the codiscoverer, along with James D. Watson, of the molecular structure of DNA. He received the Nobel Prize in 1962 for his work.

Dolly: A Finn Dorset sheep, Dolly was the first mammal to be cloned from an adult cell. Dolly developed arthritis at 5 years old, an unusually young age, and died in 2003 when she was 6, a very young age for a sheep. Some speculate that she may have been susceptible to premature aging due to the fact that her donor cell came from a 6-year-old sheep, theorizing that her cells were already 6 years old when she was born.

Food and Drug Administration: The Food and Drug Administration is a government agency that is responsible for ensuring the safety of drugs and the food supply.

Human Genome Project: The Human Genome Project was an international project started in 1990 whose goal was to identify all the genes in the human genome and map how they are sequenced. The project, which finished 2 years ahead of schedule in 2003, discovered there are only between 20,000 and 25,000 genes in the human genome.

Woo-Suk Hwang: Hwang is a Korean geneticist who claimed in 2004 that he was the first scientist to successfully clone a human embryo using somatic cell nuclear transfer techniques. However, in 2006 a South Korean academic panel determined that Hwang had falsified his data and had not produced any cloned embryonic stem cell lines.

Karl Illmensee: Illmensee is a Swiss scientist who claimed in 1979 that he had cloned mice. His results were not duplicated by any scientist until 1984.

Leon Kass: An American bioethicist known for his opposition to embryonic stem cell and cloning research, Kass is a member and former chair of the President's Council on Bioethics.

Gregor Mendel: Mendel was an Austrian priest who studied how certain traits were inherited by peas. His work became the foundation of the study of genetics.

President's Council on Bioethics: The President's Council on Bioethics is a group of leading ethicists and researchers who advise the president on biomedical issues such as cloning, stem cell research, and gene therapy.

Raël/Raëlians: Raël is the leader of a cult in which the followers (Raëlians) claim that life on Earth was created by extraterrestrials. Raël, formerly known as Claude Vorilhon, is actively trying to clone humans.

Christopher Reeve: Reeve portrayed Superman in three movies. He was paralyzed from the neck down after he was thrown from his horse in 1994. He became a staunch supporter of stem cell research to treat spinal cord injuries.

Jeremy Rifkin: Rifkin is president of the Foundation on Economic Trends, a think tank based in Washington, D.C. He is the author of many books about the impact of science and technological change on society. He is a prominent opponent of biotechnology.

Roslin Institute: The Roslin Institute is the Scottish research facility where Ian Wilmut and his colleagues cloned Dolly, the first mammal cloned from an adult cell.

Davor Solter: Solter is an American scientist, who, along with his student James McGrath, was unsuccessful in repeating Illmensee's experiment of cloning mice. He declared in an article published by *Science* magazine, "The cloning of mammals by simple nuclear transfer is biologically impossible."

Hans Spemann: Spemann, a German embryologist and Nobel Prize laureate, is called the Father of Cloning. He first proposed the "fantastical" experiment of somatic cell nuclear transfer in 1938.

Craig Venter: Venter is a biologist who founded and is the former president of Celera Genomics, a company that was in a race with the Human Genome Project to identify and sequence the human genome.

James D. Watson: Along with Francis Crick, Watson discovered the structure of the DNA molecule. Watson, Crick, and molecular biologist Maurice Wilkins were awarded the Nobel Prize in 1962 for their DNA discoveries.

Irv Weissman: A pioneering researcher in the area of stem cells, Weissman is the director of Stanford's Institute for Cancer and Stem Cell Biology.

Ian Wilmut: Wilmut is a Scottish researcher who led the team of scientists who cloned Dolly, the first mammal to be cloned from an adult cell.

Panayiotis (Panos) Zavos: A former associate of Severino Antinori, Zavos is a leading scientist in stem cell research. He also claims to have cloned humans and has published photographs in national scientific magazines of what he says is a four-day-old cloned embryo.

Chronology

1863
Gregor Mendel discovers that traits are inherited through discrete, independent units (genes) and in specific, predictable patterns.

1938
Spemann proposes a "fantastical" experiment in which the nucleus of one organism is transferred to an egg that has had its nucleus removed (called somatic cell nuclear transfer, or cloning).

1984
Danish embryologist Steen Wiladsen clones a sheep using embryonic cells.

1903
The word *clone* is coined to refer to "any group of cells or organisms produced asexually from a single sexually produced ancestor."

1906
The term *genetics* is introduced.

1981
The first in vitro fertilization clinic opens in the United States.

1875   1905   1935   1965   1995

1902
German scientist Hans Spemann uses a strand of hair to separate a two-celled salamander embryo. Each cell grows into a healthy adult salamander.

1995
Congress passes and President Bill Clinton signs the Dickey Amendment, which bans federal funding for research involving the creation or destruction of human embryos.

1894
Hans Dreisch separates the cells of a two-celled sea urchin embryo, each of which grows into a small larva, proving that an organism's entire genetic makeup is in each cell and is not diluted during the cell division process.

1952
Scientists Robert Briggs and Thomas King perform the first somatic cell nuclear transfer experiment in which they clone a frog.

1978
Louise Brown, the first "test-tube baby," is born in Great Britain. Her birth is the beginning of in vitro fertilization.

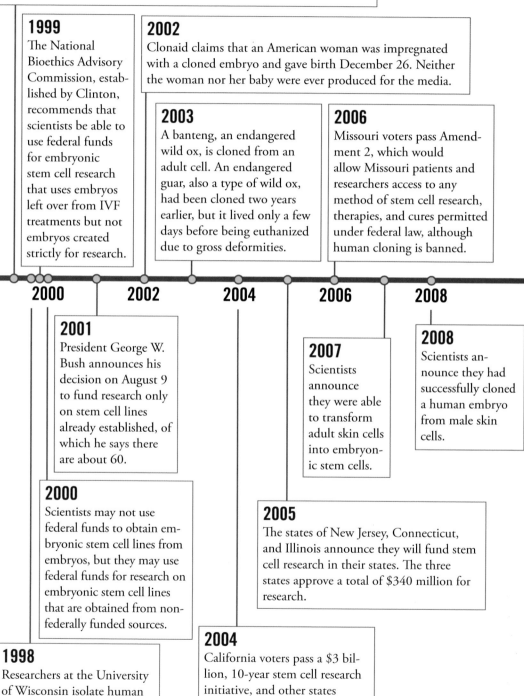

1996
Dolly, the first mammal cloned using somatic cell nuclear transfer, is born, although her birth is not announced until six months later in 1997.

1999
The National Bioethics Advisory Commission, established by Clinton, recommends that scientists be able to use federal funds for embryonic stem cell research that uses embryos left over from IVF treatments but not embryos created strictly for research.

2002
Clonaid claims that an American woman was impregnated with a cloned embryo and gave birth December 26. Neither the woman nor her baby were ever produced for the media.

2003
A banteng, an endangered wild ox, is cloned from an adult cell. An endangered guar, also a type of wild ox, had been cloned two years earlier, but it lived only a few days before being euthanized due to gross deformities.

2006
Missouri voters pass Amendment 2, which would allow Missouri patients and researchers access to any method of stem cell research, therapies, and cures permitted under federal law, although human cloning is banned.

2000 2002 2004 2006 2008

2001
President George W. Bush announces his decision on August 9 to fund research only on stem cell lines already established, of which he says there are about 60.

2007
Scientists announce they were able to transform adult skin cells into embryonic stem cells.

2008
Scientists announce they had successfully cloned a human embryo from male skin cells.

2000
Scientists may not use federal funds to obtain embryonic stem cell lines from embryos, but they may use federal funds for research on embryonic stem cell lines that are obtained from non-federally funded sources.

2005
The states of New Jersey, Connecticut, and Illinois announce they will fund stem cell research in their states. The three states approve a total of $340 million for research.

1998
Researchers at the University of Wisconsin isolate human embryonic stem cells.

2004
California voters pass a $3 billion, 10-year stem cell research initiative, and other states consider following suit.

Related Organizations

Advanced Cell Technology
One Innovation Dr., Biotech Three
Worcester, MA 01605
phone: (508) 756-1212
fax: (508) 756-4468
Web site: www.advancedcell.com

Advanced Cell Technology, Inc. is a leading biotechnology company in the emerging field of regenerative medicine. Its focus is on cloning technology for the production of young cells for the treatment of cell degenerative diseases. Its Web site provides links to many scientific articles on cloning.

American Society of Law, Medicine, and Ethics (ASLME)
765 Commonwealth Ave., Suite 1634
Boston, MA 02215
phone: (617) 262-4990
fax: (617) 437-7596
Web site: www.aslme.org

The society's members include physicians, attorneys, health-care administrators, and others interested in the relationship between law, medicine, and ethics. It takes no positions but acts as a forum for discussion of issues such as cloning. The organization has an information clearinghouse and a library. It publishes the quarterlies *American Journal of Law* and *Journal of Law, Medicine, and Ethics*; the periodic ASLME Briefings; and books.

Center for Bioethics and Human Dignity
2065 Half Day Rd.
Bannockburn, IL 60015
phone: (847) 317-8180
fax: (847) 317-8101
Web site: cbhd.org
e-mail: info@cbhd.org

The center works to help individuals and organizations address the pressing bioethical challenges of the day, including genetic intervention and reproductive technologies. It opposes cloning, human genetic modification, and embryonic stem cell research. The center publishes many position papers and editorials on its Web site.

Center for Biomedical Ethics

PO Box 33 UMHC
Minneapolis, MN 55455
phone: (612) 625-4917
Web site: www.bioethics.umn.edu

The center seeks to advance and disseminate knowledge concerning ethical issues in health care and the life sciences. It conducts original research, offers educational programs, fosters public discussion and debate, and assists in the formulation of public policy. The center publishes the quarterly newsletter *Bioethics Examiner*, the monograph *Human Stem Cells*, and overviews on human cloning and stem cells.

Center for Food Safety

660 Pennsylvania Ave. SE, #302
Washington, DC 20003
phone: (202) 547-9359
fax: (202) 547-9429
e-mail: office@centerforfoodsafety.org
Web site: www.centerforfoodsafety.org

The center is a nonprofit public interest and environmental advocacy membership that challenges harmful food production technologies and promotes sustainable alternatives. The center maintains numerous articles and fact sheets about animal cloning and food safety on its Web site.

Center for Genetics and Society

436 14th St., Suite 700
Oakland, CA 94612
phone: (510) 625-0819
fax: (510) 625-0874
Web site: www.genetics-and-society.org

The center encourages responsible uses and effective societal governance of new human genetic and reproductive technologies. It supports benign and beneficent medical applications of the new human genetic and reproductive technologies and opposes those applications that objectify and commodify human life and threaten to divide human society. The center publishes a newsletter, and its Web site provides information on government technology policies, media coverage of bioethics issues, and other topics.

Clone Rights United Front/Clone Rights Action Center

506 Hudson St.
New York, NY 10014
phone: (212) 255-1439
fax: (212) 463-0435
e-mail: r.wicker@verizon.net
Web site: www.clonerights.org

The Clone Rights United Front began as a one-issue reproductive rights organization. It was organized to oppose legislation that would make cloning a human being a felony. It is dedicated to the principle that reproductive rights, including cloning, are guaranteed by the Constitution, and that each citizen has the right to decide if, when, and how to reproduce. Its Web site has links to congressional testimony opposing a ban on human cloning and editorials supporting cloning.

Food and Drug Administration (FDA)

5600 Fishers Ln.
Rockville, Maryland 20857
phone: (888) 463-6332
Web site: www.fda.gov

The FDA ensures the safety of the nation's food supply. It also oversees feed and drugs given to pets and farm animals. In conjunction with the Center for Veterinary Medicine (CVM), the FDA studied animal cloning and food safety for seven years before releasing its final report *Animal Cloning: A Risk Assessment*, which is available on its Web site.

The Genetics and Public Policy Center
1717 Massachusetts Ave. NW, Suite 530
Washington, DC 20036
phone: (202) 663-5971
fax: (202) 663-5992
e-mail: inquiries@DNApolicy.org
Web site: www.DNApolicy.org

The Genetics and Public Policy Center was established as an independent and objective source of credible information on genetic technologies and genetic policies for the public, media, and policy makers. The center undertakes public opinion polls concerning reproductive genetic technology, and its Web site includes the article "The Regulatory Environment for Human Cloning."

National Institutes of Health (NIH)
9000 Rockville Pike
Bethesda, MD 20892
phone: (301) 4496-4000
Web site: www.stemcells.nih.gov

The NIH is the federal government's primary agency for the support of biomedical research. It is the government agency responsible for developing guidelines for research on stem cells. Its Web site includes numerous links to articles about stem cell research and frequently asked questions.

National Right to Life Committee (NRLC)
512 10th St. NW
Washington, DC 20004
phone: (202) 626-8800
e-mail: nrlc@nrlc.org
Web site: www.nrlc.org

NRLC opposes abortion and campaigns against embryonic stem cell research on the basis that the embryo is a human life that should be granted the same protections as living persons. NRLC publishes the brochures *When Does Life Begin?* and *Abortion: Some Medical Facts.*

President's Council on Bioethics

1801 Pennsylvania Ave. NW, Suite 700
Washington, DC 20006
phone: (202) 296-4669
e-mail: info@bioethics.gov
Web site: www.bioethics.gov

The council advises the president of the United States on ethical issues related to advances in biomedical science and technology. Its reports include the books *Human Cloning and Human Dignity: An Ethical Inquiry* and *Being Human: Readings from the President's Council on Bioethics.*

Stem Cell Research Foundation (SCRF)

22512 Gateway Center Dr.
Clarksburg, MD 200871
phone: (877) 842-3442
Web site: www.stemcellresearchfoundation.org

SCRF supports innovative clinical stem cell therapy research. The foundation's goal is to educate the public about and conduct fund-raising for stem cell research. It publishes a newsletter, an annual report, and the brochure *Stem Cell Research: A Revolution in Medicine.*

U.S. Conference of Catholic Bishops

3211 4th St. NE
Washington, DC 20017-1194
phone: (202) 541-3000
fax: (202) 541-3054
e-mail: pro-life@usccb.org
Web site: www.usccb.org

The U.S. Conference of Catholic Bishops advocates a legislative ban and restrictions on abortion. Its publications include the bulletin *Stem Cell Research and Human Cloning* and the brochure *A People of Life.*

For Further Research

Books

Elaine Dewar, *The Second Tree: Stem Cells, Clones, and Chimeras, and Quests for Immortality.* New York: Carroll and Graf, 2004.

Karl Drlica, *Understanding DNA and Gene Cloning.* 4th ed. Hoboken, NJ: Wiley, 2004.

Jonathan Glover, *Choosing Children: Genes, Disability, and Design.* New York: Oxford University Press, 2006.

Arlene Judith Klotzko, *A Clone of Your Own? The Science and Ethics of Cloning.* New York: Cambridge University Press, 2006.

Stephen E. Levick, *Clone Being: Exploring the Psychological and Social Dimensions.* Lanham, MD: Rowman & Littlefield, 2004.

Aaron D. Levine, *Cloning: A Beginner's Guide.* Oxford: OneWorld, 2007.

Kerry Lynn Macintosh, *Illegal Beings: Human Clones and the Law.* New York: Cambridge University Press, 2005.

Jane Maienschein, *Whose View of Life: Embryos, Cloning, and Stem Cells.* Cambridge, MA: Harvard University Press, 2003.

Gary Marcus, *The Birth of the Mind: How a Tiny Number of Genes Creates the Complexities of Human Thought.* New York: BasicBooks, 2004.

Bill McKibben, *Enough: Staying Human in an Engineered Age.* New York: Times, 2003.

Rose M. Morgan, *The Genetics Revolution: History, Fears, and Future of a Life-Altering Science.* Westport, CT: Greenwood Press, 2006.

Ramez Naam, *More than Human: Embracing the Promise of Biological Enhancement.* New York: Broadway Books, 2005.

Gregory E. Pence, *Cloning After Dolly: Who's Still Afraid?* Lanham, MD: Rowman & Littlefield, 2004.

Matt Ridley, *Nature via Nurture: Genes, Experience, and What Makes Us Human.* New York: HarperCollins, 2003.

Christopher Thomas Scott, *Stem Cell Now: From the Experiment That Shook the World to the New Politics of Life.* New York: Pi Press, 2006.

Pete Shanks, *Human Genetic Engineering: A Guide for the Activists, Skeptics, and the Very Perplexed.* New York: Nation, 2005.

Ian Wilmut and Roger Highfield, *After Dolly: The Uses and Misuses of Human Cloning.* New York: W.W. Norton, 2006.

Periodicals

Jessica Bennett, "A Bug's Story," *Newsweek International,* July 23, 2007.

Linda Bren, "Animal Cloning and Food Safety," *FDA Consumer,* March/April 2007.

Duncan Currie, "The Stem Cell Hard Sell," *Weekly Standard,* November 6, 2006.

Economist, "Clones to the Right of Me, Jokers to the Left: Stem Cell Research," January 13, 2007.

———, "Me Too, Too: Human Embryonic Stem Cells," November 24, 2007.

———, "Son of Frankenfood," January 18, 2008.

Michael Fumento, "Code of Silence: Another Source of Useful Stem Cells Has Been Found—and the Media and the Cloning Crowd Are Trying to Keep It Quiet," *Weekly Standard,* February 7, 2007.

Bernardine Healy, "A Stem Cell Victory," *U.S. News & World Report,* January 14, 2008.

Jerry Hirsch, "A Cloned Cheeseburger? Don't Fire Up the Coals Yet," *Los Angeles Times,* January 16, 2008.

Michael Humphrey, "Advances Don't Quell Stem-Cell Debate," *National Catholic Reporter,* January 11, 2008.

Chris Josefowicz, "Monster Mash: You Think Human-Animal Beasts Are Only a Myth? Think Again," *Current Science,* December 15, 2006.

Karen Kaplan, "Stem Cells Created Without Destroying Embryos," *Los Angeles Times,* January 11, 2008.

John F. Kavanaugh, "Cloning for Missouri," *America,* November 27, 2006.

Verlyn Klinkenborg, "Closing the Barn Door After the Cows Have Gotten Out," *New York Times,* January 23, 2008.

Michael D. Lemonick, "The Rise and Fall of the Cloning King," *Time,* January 6, 2006.

Los Angeles Times, "Labeling Clone-Free Food," January 19, 2008.

Gene Marcial, "Cytori: Stem Cells from Fat Tissue," *Business Week*, December 3, 2007.

James E. McWilliams, "Food Politics, Half Baked," *New York Times*, February 5, 2008.

Megan Miller, "Cloned Beef: It's What's for Dinner," *Popular Science*, September 2006.

National Review, "Stem-Cell Success," December 17, 2007.

New York Times, "Safe as Milk?" January 6, 2008.

Alice Park, "The Perils of Cloning," *Time*, July 10, 2006.

Ben Payntner, "The Other Other White Meat," *Wired*, November 2007.

Renuka Rayasam, "Cloning Around," *U.S. News & World Report*, January 8, 2007.

Brian Rooney and Peter Imber, "A Dog's Stem Cell Life," *ABCNews.com*, January 9, 2008.

Wesley J. Smith, "Cloning Doubletalk," *Weekly Standard*, March 26, 2007.

Brian D. Sweany, "Make That a Double: Cloning Asks for a Seat at the Dinner Table," *Texas Monthly*, May 2007.

Brian Vastag, "Sickle Save: Skin Cells Fix Anemia in Mice," *Science News*, December 8, 2007.

Will Verboven, "Make That Cloned, Please: The Benefits of Cloning Food Animals May Yet Overcome the Public's Distaste," *Western Standard*, February 12, 2007.

Washington Post, "What's the Beef?" February 1, 2008.

Rick Weiss, "European Ethics Group Opposes Food from Cloned Animals," *Washington Post*, January 18, 2008.

———, "Mature Human Embryos Created from Adult Skin Cells," *Washington Post*, January 18, 2008.

Jane Zhang, John W. Miller, and Lauren Etter, "Cloned Livestock Poised to Receive FDA Clearance," *Wall Street Journal*, January 4, 2008.

Web Sites

Americans to Ban Cloning (ABC) (www.cloninginformation.org). ABC is a coalition of organizations and individuals whose goal is to promote a comprehensive, global ban on cloning. It believes human cloning would commodify life and result in a race of second-class citizens. Its Web site offers a variety of articles, commentaries, and congressional testimony against human cloning.

Clonaid (www.clonaid.com). Clonaid was founded in 1997 by Raël, the spiritual leader of the Raëlian Movement, the world's largest UFO-related organization. Clonaid is the first company to publicly announce its attempt to clone human beings. Clonaid believes that once human cloning has been perfected, the next step is to transfer memories and personalities into the newly cloned human brain, thus allowing a person to live forever. Clonaid and Raël have published the book *Yes to Human Cloning,* which examines why cloning is a feasible science.

Coalition for the Advancement of Medical Research (CAMR) (www. camradvocacy.org/fastaction). CAMR comprises nationally recognized patient organizations, universities, scientific societies, foundations, and individuals with life-threatening illnesses and disorders who advocate for the advancement of breakthrough research and technologies in regenerative medicine—including stem cell research and somatic cell nuclear transfer—in order to cure disease and alleviate suffering. The coalition believes embryonic stem cell research must remain a legal and protected form of scientific research. Its Web site offers a variety of links to press releases, editorials, and congressional testimony in support of its views.

Human Cloning Foundation (www.humancloning.org). The foundation promotes education, awareness, and research about human cloning and other forms of biotechnology. It emphasizes the positive aspects of these new technologies. The foundation prefers to distribute its information over the Internet and requests that people refrain from contacting it directly for information. Its Web site offers a variety of resources, including essays on the benefits of human cloning, and an online newsletter, *The Cloner.*

The Reproductive Cloning Network (www.reproductivecloning.net). The Reproductive Cloning Network was established to store and review scientific resources regarding reproductive cloning. Its fundamental objective is to provide scientific information, statistics, and links to relevant companies and organizations. Its Web site provides a variety of links, articles, and resources about both human and animal cloning.

Source Notes

Overview

1. Quoted in Aaron D. Levine, *Cloning: A Beginner's Guide.* Oxford: OneWorld, 2007, p. 39.
2. Food and Drug Administration, *Animal Cloning: A Draft Risk Assessment,* December 28, 2006, p. 309.
3. Brigitte Boisselier, "Human Cloning Discussion at the UN," October 21, 2004. www.clonaid.com.
4. Bill McKibben, *Enough: Staying Human in an Engineered Age.* New York: Times, 2003, p. 128.
5. Arlene Judith Klotzko, *A Clone of Your Own? The Science and Ethics of Cloning.* New York: Cambridge University Press, 2006, p. 151.
6. President's Council on Bioethics, *Human Cloning and Human Dignity: An Ethical Inquiry.* New York: Public Affairs, 2002, p. 104.
7. President's Council on Bioethics, *Human Cloning and Human Dignity*, p. 104.
8. Robert Wachbroit, "Genetic Encores: The Ethics of Human Cloning," *Philosophy and Public Policy Quarterly*, vol. 17, no. 4, Fall 1997. www.publicpolicy.umd.edu.
9. Quoted in Elizabeth Weise, "Stem-Cell Research Gets Off to a Slow Start," *USA Today*, August 7, 2002, p. 3 A.
10. American Society for Reproductive Medicine, Ethics Committee, "Donating Spare Embryos for Embryonic Stem-Cell Research," *Fertility and Sterility*, vol. 78, no. 5, November 2002, p. 959.

Should Cloning Be Used in Animals?

11. James McGrath and Davor Solter, "Inability of Mouse Blastomere Nuclei Transferred to Enucleated Zygotes to Support Development In Vitro," *Science*, December 14, 1984, p. 1,319.

12. Quoted in Karen Kaplan, "Cloned Meat and Milk Are Safe to Eat, FDA Says," *Los Angeles Times*, January 16, 2008, p. A1.
13. Quoted in *Economist*, "Son of Frankenfood," January 19, 2008, p. 67.
14. Quoted in Pallavi Gogoi, "Why Cloning Is Worth It," *Business Week Online*, March 7, 2007, p. 8.
15. Food and Drug Administration Center for Veterinary Medicine, *Animal Cloning: A Risk Assessment*. Rockville, MD: Department of Health and Human Services, January 8, 2008, p. 12.
16. Center for Food Safety, "Cloned Animals," January 2008. www.centerforfoodsafety.org.

Is Human Cloning Ethical?

17. President's Council on Bioethics, *Human Cloning and Human Dignity*, p. xxviii.
18. Stephen Levick, with Natasha Mitchell, "Growing Up a Clone," *All in the Mind*, March 5, 2005. www.abc.net.au.
19. Julian Savulescu, with Natasha Mitchell, "Growing Up a Clone," *All in the Mind*, March 5, 2005. www.abc.net.au.
20. Klotzko, *A Clone of Your Own?* p. 151.
21. Quoted in President's Council on Bioethics, *Human Cloning and Human Dignity*, p. 23.
22. Sophia M. Kolehmainen, "Human Cloning: Brave New Mistake." www.gene-watch.org.
23. Quoted in John Tierney, "Are Scientists Playing God? It Depends on Your Religion," *New York Times*, November 20, 2007, p. F1.
24. Boisselier, "Human Cloning Discussion at the UN."

Is Embryonic Stem Cell Research Ethical?

25. Ron Reagan, "Speech to the Democratic National Convention," *New York Times*, July 17, 2004. www.nytimes.com.

26. Reagan, "Speech to the Democratic National Convention."

27. George W. Bush, "Executive Order: Expanding Approved Stem Cell Lines in Ethically Responsible Ways," June 20, 2007. www.whitehouse.gov.

28. Quoted in Rick Weiss, "Scientists Use Skin to Create Stem Cells," *Washington Post*, June 7, 2007, p. A1.

29. Quoted in Rick Weiss, "Advance May End Stem Cell Debate," *Washington Post*, November 21, 2007, p. A1.

30. *Washington Post*, "Stem Cell Breakthrough," November 24, 2007, p. A16.

31. Quoted in Malcolm Ritter, "Scientists in Japan, U.S. Report Stem Cell Breakthrough from Human Skin," *San Diego Union-Tribune*, November 20, 2007. http://signonsandiego.com.

32. Quoted in Ritter, "Scientists in Japan, U.S. Report Stem Cell Breakthrough."

33. Quoted in Karen Kaplan, "Stem Cell Milestone Achieved," *Los Angeles Times*, November 21, 2007, p. A15.

34. Quoted in Malcolm Ritter, "Analysis: Hurdles Remain for Stem Cells," *Washington Post*, November 22, 2007. www.washingtonpost.com.

35. Quoted in Ritter, "Analysis."

36. Quoted in Michael Abramowitz and Rick Weiss, "A Scientific Advance, a Political Question Mark," *Washington Post*, November 21, 2007, p. A4.

37. Quoted in Rick Weiss, "States Assess Breakthrough on Stem Cells," *Washington Post*, November 22, 2007, p. A3.

38. Quoted in Terri Somers, "Stem Cells Created Without Embryos," *San Diego Union-Tribune*, November 21, 2007. http://signonsandiego.com.

39. Quoted in Terri Somers, "Successful Embryo Cloning Documented," *San Diego Union-Tribune*, January 17, 2007. http://signonsandiego.com.

40. Quoted in Somers, "Successful Embryo Cloning Documented."

What Policies Should Govern Cloning?

41. Food and Drug Administration Center for Veterinary Medicine, *Animal Cloning*, 2008, p. 15.

42. Food and Drug Administration Center for Veterinary Medicine, *Animal Cloning*, p. 13.

43. Quoted in Kaplan, "Cloned Meat and Milk Are Safe to Eat, FDA Says," p. A19.

44. Quoted in Justin Gillis, "Clone-Generated Milk, Meat May Be Approved," *Washington Post*, October 6, 2005, p. A1.

45. Barbara A. Mikulski, "Mikulski Renews Call for Labeling of Cloned Food," January 22, 2008. http://mikulski.senate.gov.

46. *Economist*, "Son of Frankenfood?" p. 68.

47. *Washington Post*, "What's the Beef?" February 1, 2008, p. A20.

48. Quoted in Kaplan, "Cloned Meat and Milk Are Safe to Eat, FDA Says," p. A19.

49. Bill Clinton, "Remarks by the President on Cloning," March 4, 1997. www.clintonfoundation.org.

50. Quoted in John Garvish, "The Clone Wars: The Growing Debate over Federal Cloning Legislation," *Duke Law & Technology Review*, June 2001. www.law.duke.edu.

51. George W. Bush, "President Discusses Stem Cell Research," August 9, 2001. www.whitehouse.gov.

52. Robert P. George, "Snake Oil," *National Review Online*, July 28, 2004. www.nationalreview.com.

53. Jonathan D. Moreno, Sam Berger, and Alix Rogers, "Divided We Fail: The Need for National Stem Cell Funding," April 12, 2007. www.americanprogress.org.

List of Illustrations

Index

About the Author

Tamara L. Roleff is a freelance writer who lives in Southern California with her husband and three golden retrievers.

About the Author

2/01